Children and Young People Whose Behaviour is Sexually Concerning or Harmful

D1452434

by the same author

**Working with Children and Teenagers Using
Solution Focused Approaches**
Enabling Children to Overcome Challenges and Achieve their Potential
Judith Milner and Jackie Bateman
ISBN 978 1 84905 082 1
eISBN 978 0 85700 261 7

of related interest

**A Treatment Manual for Adolescents Displaying
Harmful Sexual Behaviour**
Change for Good
Eamon McCrory
Foreword by Jon Brown
Illustrated by Paula Walker-Rhymes
ISBN 978 1 84905 146 0
eISBN 978 0 85700 312 6

What Have I Done?
A Victim Empathy Programme For Young People
Pete Wallis
With Clair Aldington and Marian Liebmann
Illustrated by Emily Wallis
ISBN 978 1 84310 979 2
eISBN 978 0 85700 211 2

Changing Offending Behaviour
A Handbook of Practical Exercises and Photocopiable
Resources for Promoting Positive Change
Clark Baim and Lydia Guthrie
ISBN 978 1 84905 511 6
eISBN 978 0 85700 928 9

Children Who Commit Acts of Serious Interpersonal Violence
Messages for Best Practice
Edited by Ann Hagell and Renuka Jeyarajah-Dent
ISBN 978 1 84310 384 4
eISBN 978 1 84642 545 5

Communication Skills for Working with Children and Young People
Introducing Social Pedagogy
3rd edition
Pat Petrie
ISBN 978 1 84905 137 8
eISBN 978 0 85700 331 7

CHILDREN AND YOUNG PEOPLE

WHOSE BEHAVIOUR IS SEXUALLY CONCERNING OR HARMFUL

Assessing Risk and Developing Safety Plans

JACKIE BATEMAN
JUDITH MILNER

Jessica Kingsley *Publishers*
London and Philadelphia

Excerpts on page 30 and 118 are reproduced with kind permission of Andrew Turnell. Excerpt on page 96 is reproduced with kind permission of the Royal College of Psychiatrists.
Every effort has been made to trace copyright holders and to obtain their permission for the use of copyright material. The author and the publisher apologize for any omissions and would be grateful if notified of any acknowledgements that should be incorporated in future reprints or editions of this book.

First published in 2015
by Jessica Kingsley Publishers
73 Collier Street
London N1 9BE, UK
and
400 Market Street, Suite 400
Philadelphia, PA 19106, USA

www.jkp.com

Library of Congress Cataloging in Publication Data
Bateman, Jackie, 1973-
  Children and young people whose behaviour is sexually concerning or harmful : assessing risk and developing safety plans / Jackie Bateman and Judith Milner.
    pages cm
  Includes bibliographical references and index.
  ISBN 978-1-84905-361-7 (alk. paper)
  1. Children--Sexual behavior--Great Britain. 2. Youth--Sexual behavior--Great Britain. I. Milner, Judith, 1941- II. Title.
  HQ784.S45B38 2015
  306.708350941--dc23

                    2014027601

British Library Cataloguing in Publication Data
A CIP catalogue record for this book is available from the British Library

ISBN 978 1 84905 361 7
eISBN 978 0 85700 714 8

Printed and bound in Great Britain

CONTENTS

ACKNOWLEDGEMENTS

There are many people to whom we owe thanks:

- Lorell Webster for patiently reading drafts and her generous feedback, advice and support
- Paul Edwards for his continuous encouragement and frank comments
- Barnardo's The Junction, particularly Carol Larne and Laura Walker
- Stephen Jones at Jessica Kingsley Publishers for his encouragement and guidance.

And lastly we acknowledge the children, young people and their families who have agreed for their stories to be shared.

Introduction

About this Book

The sexual behaviour of children and young people is frequently inappropriate; sometimes concerning; and, less frequently, harmful. Yet professionals who are confident when working with problems such as challenging or offending behaviour often lose this confidence when faced with behaviour that has a sexual component. To some extent this is because a wide variety of initiatives reporting varying levels of success has contributed to a piecemeal development of risk management strategies and treatment methodologies. Rather than compare approaches or critique methodologies, this book sets out the practical application of a strengths-based approach to safety assessments and the development of safe care plans.

Whether the worker is a primary school teacher faced with a child who follows other pupils into the toilet and touches their private parts, a foster parent who discovers that her fourteen-year-old foster child has stolen her knickers from the washing basket or a social worker who is asked to deal with a young person in a residential home who has sexually assaulted younger children, this book will help that worker develop a language for talking about the behaviours, assess levels of risk and safety, and manage it through the development of safe care plans.

Using strengths-based approaches to working with children and young people, the book offers effective and creative ways of developing responsibility-taking and safety with those who deny, minimise and rationalise their behaviour, children who are both abused and abusers, and those with learning difficulties. Guidance is provided on how to talk with children and young people who may be difficult to reach because of embarrassment, shame and fear of the consequences of their behaviour. The development of safe care plans, for the home and/or school, is detailed, concentrating on areas of communication, supervision, and supportive networks. The book highlights the importance of working with families and networks, and any concomitant challenging behaviours to ensure that children develop both sexual safety for others and emotional and sexual safety for themselves.

CHAPTER 1

Myths, Realities and Possibilities

The Legal Framework

The legal framework for work with children and young people with harmful sexual behaviour was initially set out in the Children Act 1989, which required services to be provided to meet the needs of this group of young people, as children in need, under Section 17 and Schedule 2 of the Act. The first piece of guidance which specifically made reference to children and young people with harmful sexual behaviour was the second edition of *Working Together under the Children Act 1989* (Department of Health 1991), which recommended that child protection procedures should be followed with the convening of a child protection conference followed by a review on completion of a comprehensive assessment. This was swiftly followed by the semi-formal guidance set out in *The Report of the Committee of Enquiry into Children and Young People Who Sexually Abuse Other Children* (National Children's Home 1992), which provided a more comprehensive picture of how young people who were engaging in harmful sexual behaviour were being managed in the UK. The findings were not optimistic, there being:

- conflict over definitions of what constitutes juvenile sexual assault
- fewer than half of local authorities in England and Wales in 1990 had any facilities to provide treatment for young people who sexually abuse other children
- no coordinated management structure
- an absence of policy, and uncertainty about the legitimacy of the work

- clashes of philosophy, especially between juvenile justice and child protection approaches
- inadequate data about the nature, scope and effects of the problem
- an absence of internal and inter-agency policy and practice guidance
- lack of clarity about assessment and intervention models
- an absence of services for younger children
- placement problems and risks arising from victims and abusers being placed in the same accommodation
- inadequate supervision and training
- alienation of front line workers trying to tackle the problem.

The report recommended the establishment of an overall systemic approach with:

- each agency defining its responsibility
- the work located in the child protection system
- abusers not to be placed in foster care with younger children
- the work placed within the scope of area child protection committees (ACPCs) with annual reports commenting specifically on progress
- the police and social services departments (SSDs) jointly investigating such cases
- the development of a continuum of care/services ranging from local/community to secure/regional therapeutic facilities
- the development of inter-agency policies and communication
- the development through government departments of national good practice guidance
- an integrated training strategy
- research to explore incidence, causality and intervention.

A sub-group of the Inter-department Group on Child Abuse was established in recognition of the need to coordinate the work with offenders. In 1992 they published a *Strategic Statement on Working with Abusers*, which commented that:

> When another child or young person is suspected of abusing a child, child protection procedures should come into play in respect of both the victim and the alleged perpetrator...Adolescent abusers are themselves in need of services because available evidence suggests that early and appropriate intervention will bring abusive behaviour under control. (DoH 1992, p.2)

The following strategic objectives were then implemented locally through the area child protection committees (ACPCs):

- formulating a coherent policy for the management and treatment of abusers
- building a better understanding of abusers
- viewing sexual abuse as a problem requiring assessment and treatment both for the abuser and the victim
- promoting a multi-disciplinary approach to the problem
- encouraging local and national resources, in recognition of the high demands of the work
- educating both the public and professionals about this problem.

What appeared to be a comprehensive and considered response unfortunately fell down in its implementation. This was highlighted in a report by Masson (1995) who surveyed 106 area child protection committees, concluding that only 17 per cent had drawn up inter-agency procedures; 43 per cent had working parties on the issue; and different models of practice were identified which were attempting to merge child protection and youth justice policies. This compared badly with adult services where 98 per cent of probation services had strategies in place for the management of adult sex offenders (Masson 1995). The struggle to implement guidance was nicely summed up by Morrison:

> The journey from policy to practice is a long and winding one. It is a salutary reminder that isolation, and being left alone with this problem, remains the experience for many professionals, whether in social services, health or education, a process that exactly mirrors that of young abusers, their victims and the families. (Conference speech, 14 March 1996)

To complicate matters further there was an expansion in the policies and legislations regarding the general area of sexual offending in the implementation of the Sex Offenders Act 1997 (followed by the Sexual Offences Act 2003). This legislation placed a statutory responsibility on all sexual offenders, regardless of whether they were an adult or young person, to advise police of where they were living, and their names were placed on the Sex Offenders Register. The distinguishing difference between adults and young people was the registration period; for the latter it was half of that for an adult. The inclusion of young people who had sexually offended within these acts was a cause of concern:

> There is considerable concern that a number of adolescents are unnecessarily and inappropriately subjected to requirements such as sex offender registration, custodial sentencing and involvement in intensive long-term therapeutic programmes with the result that they become increasingly isolated, defensive and stigmatised. (NOTA National Committee on Adolescents Who Sexually Harm 2003)

The Sex Offenders Act (1997) was followed by the Crime and Disorder Act 1998 which, being greatly influenced by *Misspent Youth 98: The Challenge for Youth Justice* (Audit Commission 1998) and the government publication *No More Excuses* (Home Office 1997) shifted the approach to youth crime from diversion and decriminalisation to an agenda and requirement for tougher sentences and punishment, thus widening the divide between child welfare and youth justice. During the same period, *Working Together to Safeguard Children* (DoH 1999), influenced by *Messages from Research* (DoH 1995), expanded on the original guidance on the management of children and young people who sexually abuse outlined in *Working Together* (DoH 1991). The 1999 document highlighted that:

> Work with children and young people who abuse others – including those who sexually abuse/offend – should recognise that such children are likely to have considerable needs themselves... Such children and young people are likely to be children in need, and some will in addition be suffering or at risk of significant harm, and may themselves be in need of protection. (DoH: 6.31)

It specified three key principles that should be adhered to in working with children and young people who sexually harm others:

- a co-coordinated approach for all agencies involved
- the needs of the children who have abused others should be considered separately from those of their victims
- an assessment should identify any unmet developmental needs that this group of young people displays, alongside any specific needs that arise from their behaviour.

Within this guidance, the *Framework for the Assessment of Children in Need and their Families* (DoH 2000) was also referenced.

The *Framework for the Assessment of Children in Need and their Families* was introduced to address problems with the original assessment framework which had become known as the 'Orange Book' (DoH 1988) and the findings from *Messages from Research* (DoH 1995) that highlighted a significant imbalance between children who were in need of 'protection' and 'children in need'. It was intended that the new framework should provide a systematic framework for assessing children in need. Whilst there were some positives to the new framework, particularly an emphasis on placing children with their families and wider community, and identifying strengths as well as weaknesses, it failed in its application and response to children and young people who sexually abuse, particularly with regard to the inclusion of risk and harm.

The Criminal Justice Act 2003 was an additional piece of legislation that supported the creation of local multi-agency public protection arrangements (MAPPAs). This forum was designed to monitor closely and manage registered sexual offenders, including adolescent offenders.

In 2003, Hackett and Masson published the results of a two-year investigation which considered what provisions were available for this group of young people in the UK and the Republic of Ireland (RoI). The research concluded that there were nearly 200 services or projects offering intervention to sexually harming young people. Whilst the report stated that there was a much more sophisticated and professional approach to the work in the UK than the RoI, it also described service provision as being patchy and uncoordinated, and inconsistencies in the convening of child protection conferences and multi-agency meetings as well as in the effective application of the Multi-Agency Public Protection Arrangements (MAPPA). Of the theoretical models which underpinned intervention approaches, cognitive behavioural therapy was cited as the preferred model (56 per cent) (Hackett and Masson 2003). Similar themes continued to be mirrored in the Youth Justice Board's (YJB) publications *Services for Young People Who Sexually Abuse: A Report on Mapping and Exploring Services for Young People Who Have Sexually Abused Others* (Hackett, Masson and Phillips 2005), *Key Elements of Effective Practice: Young People Who Sexually Abuse* (YJB 2008), and the *UK Children's Commissioners' Report to the UN Committee on the Rights of the Child* (UK Children's Commissioners 2008). The 2013 publication, *Examining Multi-Agency Responses to Children and Young People Who Sexually Offend* (Criminal Justice Joint Inspection 2013), identified positive outcomes where agencies work together and engage with the young people, and makes reference to the effective intervention of strengths-based approaches. Nevertheless, it also highlighted missed opportunities to intervene earlier and, despite there being evidence of some good practice, more generally there was poor communication between agencies, inadequate assessments and a lack of evaluation at a strategic level.

As is evident from this brief summary of the policy, legislation and studies related to this area of work, there have been considerable shifts in legislation, underlying philosophy and practice intervention with regard to the management of this group of young people. It is interesting, however, that salient messages and guidance that were being provided in the early 1990s regarding a coordinated and coherent response remain outstanding.

The knowledge base

More than any other challenging behaviour, the sexual abuse of one child by another generates anxiety, puzzlement and confusion. Dealing with a defiant or delinquent child may be difficult but most adults have a clear idea of what they should be doing about it. This confidence seems to leave them when confronted with sexual misbehaviour. This is partly because of notions of the innocent, and by implication, asexual child until adolescence, although the child's natural curiosity might lead to some harmless experimentation. As sexual activity with any child under the age of 16 is potentially a criminal offence (Sexual Offences Act 2003), what is to be made of a child who is found to be not only sexually active but also sexually harmful to other children? Hackett (2004) estimated that up to 20 per cent of all sexual offending is committed by young people who are below the age of criminal responsibility. In the absence of an existing knowledge base, professionals turned to research findings on adults who had been convicted of sexual offences to explain young people's behaviour and devise interventions to prevent them re-offending.

In the 1980s, the main studies of harmful sexual behaviour were those searching for predictive risk factors in convicted adult offenders of serious sexual assaults on children and young people. These studies identified youthful onset of sexualised behaviour as the major factor common to serious sexual offenders (for an overview, see Hanson 2004). This fuelled concerns that youthful harmful sexual behaviour was more serious than other delinquent behaviours in that it had a strong potential to develop into serious sexual offending in adulthood. However, extrapolating research findings from a high-risk, atypical group has the effect of over-identifying 'dangerousness'. For example, as Chaffin (2008) asks, in finding an association between chronic heroin addiction and reported use of cannabis in adolescence, do we then make the assumption that all adolescents caught smoking cannabis should be viewed as potential chronic heroin users and subsequently initiate 'methadone' programmes for them? Similarly, Greenland's (1987) influential study of child abuse and neglect found that being a mother, particularly a single mother, was a predictive factor in cases of neglect, so should all single mothers be classified as a potential risk to their children? As Parton (1990) pointed out, as women do most of the caring, this finding is hardly surprising. Viewing sexualised behaviour as different from, and more dangerous than, other childhood behaviours led to it being seen as requiring specialised expertise.

Despite the identification of some predictive risk factors in incarcerated serious sex offenders, very little was actually known about adult offenders in general. No single factor was found to be sufficient to predict recidivism (Christodoulides *et al.* 2005) and due to the heterogeneous nature of this group of offenders, there was no consistent profile of the sex offender (Craig *et al.* 2005). The identified risk factors were all static and enduring so of little use in designing intervention programmes, which were highly experimental. Nevertheless, the dominant approach for youthful offenders in the 1980s was to adapt models used with adults:

> There is an acceptance that adolescent sex abusers have developed a dysfunctional behaviour which is not generally mitigated by time alone. The deviant behaviours and thinking processes of the abusers originate from negative experiences, such as various forms of abuse in childhood, which lead to the abuser developing deep needs for power, acceptance and aggression which they meet through abusive sexual behaviour. The secrecy, perceived sense of power, arousal and masturbation to deviant fantasies may then serve to reinforce the abusive behaviour to the extent that it becomes compulsive. (O'Callaghan and Print 1994, p.156)

Not surprisingly, these programmes were based predominately on cognitive behavioural approaches; for example, the four preconditions model (Finkelhor 1984) and the sexual abuse cycle (Wolf 1984; Lane and Zamora 1982, 1984; Lane 1991, 1997). These two models became popular in the UK as, although separate models, they are complementary to each other in many ways, particularly the attempt to explain both the development of the behaviour and the process whereby the offence takes place (for a fuller discussion, see Fisher 1994). Even though dynamic risk factors were not fully understood (see Hanson 2004), programmes attempted to target them by adopting an eclectic methodology. For example, the G-map Programme was based on humanistic *and* cognitive restructuring therapies (O'Callaghan and Print 1994).

The late 1990s saw a significant increase in the number of studies which identified more positive outcomes for this group of young people. Research by Polaschek (2001) and Vivian-Byrne (2002) questioned the effectiveness of confrontational conventional cognitive behavioural interventions that focused exclusively on sexual offending. Hackett (2004) found that such approaches had limited effectiveness with young people who engage in sexual offending and that offence-focused or related group treatment programmes failed to address the therapeutic needs that many sexually abusive adolescents display (see also, Richardson 2005). A significant development was the conjecture around recidivism, with later studies concluding that the vast majority of young people who engage in harmful sexual behaviour are unlikely to re-offend sexually (Worling and Curwen 2000; Caldwell 2002;

Reitzel and Carbonell 2006; McCann and Lussier 2008; Caldwell 2010). These findings challenged previous dominant assumptions that young people are more likely to grow into their offending behaviour. Indeed, they are very much more likely to grow out of it.

Rather than focusing exclusively on the harmful sexual behaviour, strengths-based assessment and intervention approaches have become increasingly recognised, as has an appreciation of the wider agenda, with the need to include offenders' families within the work and an increased understanding of how a young person is engaging with society. Unfortunately, whilst great strides have been made in therapeutic responses to this group of young people, this appears not to have reduced public concerns and anxieties. There remains a polarisation between the facts we do know and the misconceptions of what we think we know. We address these below.

Myths and realities
HOW RISKY IS THIS BEHAVIOUR?

Professionals' concerns that children who sexually harm other children are likely to develop and increase their sexual (mis)behaviour into adulthood are not borne out as an increasing number of longitudinal studies have become available (Grubin 1998; Alexander 1999; Caldwell 2002). It has become clearer that children do respond to a variety of interventions to manage and change their behaviour, and that these interventions are generally effective in preventing the recurrence of such behaviour (Carpentier, Silovsky and Chaffin 2006). Unfortunately, despite these data there still remains an unwarranted perception of high levels of risk in the minds of many people; parents frequently tell us that they had to move house after it was discovered that their child had sexually harmed another. Later in the book we explain how to assess both risk and safety at individual family and community levels, and develop safety plans.

It is often thought that young people who engage in harmful sexual behaviour are more dangerous than the general juvenile offending population. However, research undertaken by Carpentier *et al.* (2006) and Caldwell (2007) concluded that statistically, the difference between these two groups was not significant. In fact, Caldwell discovered that on release from custody it was the non-sexual offenders that engaged in future sexual offending at a significantly greater percentage (85 per cent) than those previously incarcerated for sexual offences. Yet this research finding is not reflected in public policy, and often what happens is that pathologising and totalising descriptions of young people as sexual offenders become the norm. This in turn can restrict their development and the social context of their lives at a time when they are negotiating and constructing their identities. This contradiction between research and public policy is clearly reflected in the Sex Offenders Act 1997 and the Sexual Offences Act 2003 where both adult and juvenile offenders follow the same registration process. Longo and Calder argued that 'these laws may go on to not only damage these young lives, but also further delay their individual potential for healthy recovery' (2005, p.340).

In contrast, where young people who have displayed sexually concerning behaviour have supportive families, friends and social activities, and the young person is grounded in the community and feelings of belonging, sexual safety is increased. These *social anchors*, argue Sampson and Laub (2005), significantly reduce the likelihood of recidivism.

ARE THEY A DISTINCT GROUP OF YOUNG PEOPLE?

Another assumption which has had a bearing on policy and practice issues is that young people who engage in this behaviour are one homogeneous group, particularly that the behaviour follows a predictable pattern and is characterised by cognitive distortions which are fuelled by deviant sexual fantasies. It is now recognised and supported by stronger empirical research that heterogeneity does not exist within this population (see, for example, Ryan *et al.* 1996; McCrory 2010). There are some commonalities; it is inevitable that there may be factors such as domestic violence, attachment and parental capacity which are reflective and repetitive across the lives of some young people and which also have a bearing on the development and maintenance of their sexually concerning behaviour – troubled children are usually troublesome too. However, it is now recognised that for others, these factors will have had no significance in their motivation. This in itself evidences the importance of recognising that no one programme fits all and that programmes should be reflective of individual needs and identify levels of safety within the assessment process.

CAN THESE YOUNG PEOPLE CHANGE?

Children and young people who sexually harm other children do respond to a variety of interventions to manage and change their behaviour, and these interventions are generally effective in preventing the recurrence of such behaviour (Carpentier *et al.* 2006). They do not necessarily need to be long-term, high intensity programmes. Studies by Silovsky *et al.* (2007) concluded that childhood sexual behaviour problems improve naturally with no treatment, although treatment accelerates this improvement and treatment type does appear to matter for achieving long-term success, individually tailored strengths-based interventions targeted at keeping offenders and their victims safe being the most effective.

Possibilities

Strengths-based approaches that have been found effective in working with young people who display harmful sexual behaviour share two basic premises: (1) everyone and their environments have strengths, skills and abilities but which may have been forgotten or the individual is struggling to use them at their full potential, and (2) all people have the potential for change (Rapp 1998; Early and GlenMaye 2000). The link between these two premises is important, says Saleebey: 'It is as wrong to deny the problem as it is to deny the possible!' (2013, p.270). The identification of strengths on its own does not indicate that there is safety; it is how the strengths are used to promote and effect change that can be used to assess safety. Strengths-based approaches also make clear precisely what changes would be expected if a problem is deemed to be solved. Saleebey (2007) suggests that it is as important to design a diagnostic strengths manual as it is to list the diagnoses of problems. For example, he proposes that the condition of trustworthiness could be diagnosed by the following criteria – for at least six months, nearly every day, the individual has exhibited at least three of the following:

- did what he or she promised
- kept at a task that has many snares and difficulties
- did not reveal a confidence
- stuck by a relative, friend or colleague during a rough time
- did more than was expected.

✐ **PRACTICE ACTIVITY**

How would you diagnose respectfulness? List five characteristics by which respectfulness could be measured.

Strengths models

The major assessment and intervention methods using a strengths approach include: the good lives model, narrative therapy, resilience models and solution-focused approaches. Each model is briefly discussed below.

THE GOOD LIVES MODEL

This model was developed in the first decade of the 21st century, largely for work with sexually offending behaviours (Ward 2002; Ward and Stewart 2003; Ward and Mann 2004; Ward, Mann and Gannon 2007). Its main contribution is the way in which it applies positive psychology, the study of human happiness and mental wellness, to problematic behaviour. It also provides a different orientation between worker and service user. In this model, human wellbeing requires the achievement of at least eight *primary goods*:

- life – optimal functioning physically, sexually, mentally and socially
- knowledge
- excellence – a level of mastery/agency at play and work (autonomy and self-directedness)
- inner peace – free of turmoil, stress, conflict
- relatedness/friendship – belonging, being intimate, family, community
- spirituality – in the broad sense of finding meaning and purpose in life
- happiness
- creativity.

These primary goods are the foundation of wellbeing and of a clear sense of identity and therefore in the best interest of the individual and the community. What we all hope to achieve is a good life, one that optimises our sense of wellbeing. However, whilst the pursuit of primary goods is to be supported, the means have to be socially acceptable, and unacceptable, disrespectful and unsafe means are to be challenged. Challenges are not confrontational as the style of the model is supportive of the person, looking at their strengths and abilities, examining in some detail how they go about achieving other primary goods. A holistic view is sought, strengths are mobilised and built on and the pursuit of a good life is encouraged throughout. Negative language is avoided as much as possible – words such as 'distortion', 'irrational' and 'deviant' are replaced with 'change of life', 'new approach', 'self-management', 'intimacy building' and 'healthy functioning'.

The focus on the offender's best interests and good intentions means that it is easier to avoid moral condemnation of *the person*; because their behaviour is harmful, it is *means* rather than intentions that are being challenged. This enables an empathic working relationship to be maintained. It is claimed that this accounts for greater motivation on the part of offenders and more persistence with the work. The past and its meaning are explored to understand their influence and the obstacles they place in the person's way.

In this approach assessment starts with the present situation but soon broadens out to look at the person's pursuit of primary goods as a whole. It establishes:

- what is important to the person, what their priorities are for the attainment of wellbeing

- what lacks or influences tempted them to take the unsatisfactory direct routes or shortcuts

- risk to others – need and responsibility are explored as the person is invited to draw his/her own conclusions during a joint investigative conversation

- strengths and life achievements – how can the person become more fulfilled and what goals would promote this?

The intentions and rationale of the worker are to be transparent, namely to work out how to get the person to achieve a fulfilling life, as this is seen as the best safeguard for the future. The link between the offending behaviour and a specific good is examined, as well as the details of daily living and how this might be relating to other goods, or not, as a picture of the person's relationships and environment emerges, and in particular how they see themselves *vis-à-vis* various primary and secondary goods:

- What is important to them and how do they go about getting it?
- What else do they hope to achieve in the future? Are there cognitive processes that need to be changed?
- Is there an overarching good or value that sums up the person?
- Could that be a focus to begin with?

For a fully worked case study using the good lives model with a teenager who sexually assaulted a mentally confused young woman, see Wylie and Griffin (2013).

RESILIENCE MODEL

Positive psychology also underpins this model but rather than primary goods, the emphasis is on the skills and characteristics that make some children more resilient than others (Reivich and Shatte 2003; Selekman 2002, 2007). Some young people cope with setbacks very well, whether they are small ones, such as not being picked for the school football team, or big ones, such as living in a home where there is domestic violence. Their resilience helps them pick themselves up and get on with life. A growing body of research and practice shows that most people overcome serious adversity; particularly demanding and stressful experiences do not lead inevitably to vulnerability, failure to adapt and psychopathology (for an overview, see Saleebey 2013). Others don't cope at all well; they get stuck, see life as very unfair and sometimes become depressed or begin harming themselves or others. The difference between these two groups of children is not the severity of their problems; it is the ability to get a good outcome in the face of adversity. Research on resilience has argued for a shift in our attention from the traditional focus on an individual's deficits to engaging individuals in the identification of strengths in times of difficulty (see, for example, Luthar, Cicchetti and Becker 2000;

Edwards and Pedrotti 2004). Saleebey (2007, p.285) maintains that all environments, however bleak, have resources that can be used to develop resilience skills.

Having a sense of humour is probably the most important resilience skill but as it can't be learned, learnable resilience skills form the focus of resilience approaches. These include:

- *emotional awareness*: the ability to identify what you are feeling and, when necessary, the ability to control your feelings

- *impulse control*: the ability to tolerate ambiguity so that you don't rush to make decisions, rather to look at things thoughtfully

- *optimism wedded to reality*: not simply looking on the 'bright side' all the time, but an optimistic, explanatory style that helps you think about adverse experiences in a constructive way – i.e. as a temporary setback

- *the ability to look at problems from many perspectives*

- *the ability to read and understand emotions*: a social competence that provides social support

- *not necessarily going it alone*: knowing when to ask for help and where to go for that help

- *self-efficacy*: confidence in your own ability to solve problems, knowing your strengths and weaknesses, and relying on the former to cope

- *reaching out*: being prepared to take appropriate risk, willing to try things and considering failure as a part of life.

Although most people have a self-righting tendency, it needs to be supported by internal and external factors as resilience is dependent on the interaction of factors at all levels of life. Earlier we touched briefly on the importance of supportive families, friends, social activities and the young person feeling they are a valued member of the community as important factors in reducing sexual re-offending. These are some of the characteristics of resilience:

- *Having a support network of family, friends and teachers* is an important component of resilience: 'many of life's major resiliences are acquired in the context of close relationships, particularly parent–child and peer relationships' (Howe 2008, p.107). Although resilience is mostly learned in a family environment that is low in criticism and high in warmth, somewhat surprisingly, children lacking these basics develop resilience where they have support in at least one aspect of a possible network. In his chapter in *The Child's World*, Gilligan (2010) comments that just one committed adult and/or a good school experience is a source of resilience for children. Equally, friends are very important in childhood and can provide a support network for children lacking this at home.

- *Confidence that they can face new and challenging situations.* This confidence develops from previous successes that remind children of how they have overcome adversity in the past.

- *Having a sense of purpose and future.* Having ambitions, goals, a desire for achievement, and motivation helps children believe that things will be better in the future.

- *Socially competent children* who are friendly and have a sense of humour also have resilience because they are active and adaptable as well as having supportive friends.

- *Problem-solving skills* are also a key characteristic as then the child can reflect on problems, using flexibility and willingness to attempt alternative solutions.

- *Autonomy.* Resilient children have a sense of their own identity and an ability to exert some control over their own environment. Interestingly, some children in dysfunctional families separate themselves psychologically from their families and this resilience is a safeguarding factor.

- *Attitudes* are also important as children who can stay involved rather than withdraw are more likely to be able to keep trying to influence events rather than give up. They also learn that stress is a challenge to be faced rather than bemoan their fate. This involves seeing themselves accurately so that they can distinguish between problems that are their own fault, take responsibility to try to correct the behaviour and still feel worthwhile when problems are not their fault (Selekman 2007).

The characteristics of resilience add up to what has been called social capital: 'Social relationships and a sense of emotional connectedness with others appears to bring great social benefits' (Howe 2008, p.178). This model looks at developing resilience so that young people who sexually harm others can contain and regulate their feelings so that they can stay connected with others.

For more information on how to use a resilience approach in working with young offenders, see Clark (2013).

NARRATIVE THERAPY

The approach is more overtly political, cultural and social than other approaches in that it is concerned about the oppressive effects of dominant narratives on people's understanding of the validity of their ways of living (White 1993, 1995; White and Epston 1990; Epston 1998; Payne 2006). White (1995) argues that there isn't a single story of life that is free of ambiguity and contradiction and can handle all the contingencies of life. These ambiguities, contradictions and contingencies stretch our meaning-making resources, especially when there are dominant cultural stories about particular sorts of behaviour. These stories tend to concentrate on identifying the behaviours seen as desirable by the most powerful groups of people, thus people whose behaviour does not conform to this become storied as deficient in some way. White refers to this as being entered into a story, a story which people come to believe about themselves, and one which the professional may unconsciously perpetuate:

> Labels always bespeak the reality of an outsider, they collectivize and abstract real experience, and make the client's own experience and stories seem alien and contrived. We must use labels judiciously if at all with a profound respect for their distortions and limitations. (Saleebey 2007, p.269)

In narrative assessments the problem is first deconstructed. This takes the form of searching for *unique outcomes* or *sparkling moments* (Bird 2000) – times when the young person actively resisted the influence of the problem, a contradiction to the dominant story, or 'plot' in Epston's terms (1998, p.11). Deconstructing the problem is done by reflecting with young people how they came to be recruited into a *problem-saturated story* in which they are often vilified (Augusta-Scott 2007). This includes discussing that story in a way that separates the problem from the person, developing a sense of alienation between the person and the problem. This *externalising* conversation is helped by asking questions that establish the influence of the problem on the person, and their influence on it. This can be seen as discussing the person's relationship *with* the problem. Separating the person from the problem enables the young person and the professional to work together to remove the problem. Externalising conversations are a particularly useful way of engaging with young people who sexually harm others, who understandably rarely want to talk about what they have done. Young children are often able to discuss ways of talking about their problem when it has a name chosen by the child, such as *'the touching problem'* (Myers, McLaughlin and Warwick 2003) or 'Mr Just Do It' (Milner 2008).

White (1996) states very clearly that while the alternative narrative offered may be seen as part of radical constructionism he does not accept that 'anything goes' simply by giving it a new name. Because narrative is constitutive of people's lives, shaping and structuring them, we must be accountable to those we seek to assess or help. Not all stories are equally good in their effects. Payne (2006) discusses the implications for workers of deconstructing their own stories. While he acknowledges that racism and patriarchy are cultural beliefs rejected by most of us, he reminds us of the need for constant vigilance against the more subtle manifestations of these stories; for example, the way sexism may be demonstrated through verbal tone and the dominance of conversations. Jenkins (1996) refers to this as the danger of acting from a position of self-righteousness and moral superiority. In narrative assessments, therefore, critical self-monitoring and regular checking out with other people is essential.

Having been invited to explore the effects of the problem – for example, 'I might get locked up' or 'I have to have a teacher with me all the time' – the young person is then asked if that is something they want in their lives or not (an evaluation of the problem or their relationship with it). If they do not want it, they are asked to justify that evaluation by explaining, for example, reasons for not wanting it, and what it then says about them as people. In this way they make a decision to start reclaiming their life from the influence of the problem and this clearly makes for a promising assessment. In working with harmful sexual behaviour, beliefs and attitudes which may be supporting the violence are also externalised, *externalising the internalised story*, enabling other ways of responding to situations to be discovered. Jenkins (1990, 1996) suggests that much male violence is supported by dominant stories about 'being a man' in which the need to 'be someone' is exaggerated and extreme.

For a fully worked case example, see Myers *et al.* (2003).

SOLUTION-FOCUSED SAFETY APPROACHES

One way in which strengths can become central to conversations with young people who sexually harm others is by using solution-focused questions. The solution-focused approach was developed through talking with people and asking them what works best for them, keeping these suggestions and discarding any others (de Shazer 1985, 1988, 1991). Solution-focused conversations aim to re-ignite a person's problem-solving potential and activate their own internal resources or resourcefulness. In the context of harmful sexual behaviour this approach looks at the times when the young person could have exhibited sexualised behaviour but didn't (exceptions to the problem), using the child's strengths and resources to build on these so that safety is increased.

Turnell and Edwards (1999) devised a Signs of Safety approach as a comprehensive (risk) assessment which documents both concerns and safety alongside canvassing the goals and perspectives of both professionals and family members. The practice principles of the Signs of Safety approach outlined by Turnell and Edwards (1999) have been helpful in developing an assessment process:

- understanding the position of each family member
- finding exceptions to the problem
- discovering family strengths and resources
- focusing on goals
- scaling safety and progress
- assessing willingness, confidence and capacity.

The Signs of Safety approach is used in many child protection services across the world and is flexible enough to accommodate other cultures.

In addition, the framework was further developed to include denied child abuse (Turnell and Essex 2006), and is constantly updated via the Signs of Safety website.[1]

The approach is about monitoring, maintaining and building upon levels of safety rather than risk as no assessment tools are adequate in their measurement of risk and don't indicate or provide direction about how to manage it. The issue of risk is highlighted in the Munro Report (2011) with recognition that risk can never be eradicated and needs to be managed effectively. This is not to say that risk is ignored; the framework simultaneously explores harm and danger at the same time as eliciting strengths and enquiring into safety. In a Signs of Safety risk assessment, there are four domains of enquiry:

- What are we worried about? (past harm, future danger and complicating factors)

- What's working well? (existing strengths and safety)

- What needs to happen? (future safety)

- Where are we on a scale of 0–10 where 10 means there is enough safety to be confident to close the case and 0 means it is certain that a child will be re-abused? (judgement).

(Turnell 2012, p.27)

The assessment is presented as a one-page safety plan that is clear to professionals and family, and involves them fully. The safety plan is 'a specific set of rules and arrangements that describe how the family will go about and live its everyday life that shows everyone, the professionals and the family's own support people that the children will be safe in the future' (Turnell 2012, p.37). The plan is monitored and refined over time. Safety plans can be devised for situations outside ordinary family life; for example, plans can be made for a safe classroom involving the participation of pupils as well as teachers and parents. Similarly safety in children's homes can be drawn up between care home workers, children, and visiting professionals.

For fully worked case examples, see Turnell and Essex (2006).

---

1   www.signsofsafety.net

Summary

The reasons why young people harm others sexually, how likely they are to continue in these behaviours and what interventions work are now better understood. Although most young people grow out of harmful sexual behaviour, others benefit from interventions based on strengths approaches. Four such approaches have been very briefly described: the good lives model, resilience approaches, narrative therapy, and solution-focused safety approaches.

Although distinct in how interventions are devised, the models share many similarities, particularly how existing strengths can be utilised and developed to facilitate change through collaborative relationships. All four models emphasise the crippling effects of labelling (for an overview, see Saleebey 2013). Although elements of each model are described differently, they also have similarities; for example, the characteristics of resilience resonate with the primary goods of the good lives model, and the sparkling moments/unique outcomes of narrative therapy are not dissimilar to the exception finding in solution-focused safety approaches. All models are used to challenge delicately, respectfully and supportively. In applying these models to the assessment and intervention of harmful sexual behaviour, risk is not ignored. It is only where strengths are utilised to develop measurable protective factors that safety can be assessed.

The strengths models briefly outlined in this chapter are used in the assessment and intervention of youthful harmful sexual behaviour at all levels of severity. For example, the good lives model has been adopted for use in young offender institutions (see, for example Ward and Stewart 2003; Ward et al. 2007) and specialist residential care homes such as those provided by Northern Care;[2] narrative therapy and solution-focused safety approaches have been adopted for work with young people who remain in their communities (Myers et al. 2003; Myers and Milner 2007). Our direct experience is with solution-focused safety and narrative models and this is the model we describe and illustrate throughout the rest of the book.

---

2   www.northern-care.co.uk

CHAPTER 2

Developing Safety Through Strengths and Solution Talk

This chapter introduces the basic practice principles of the solution-focused approach and begins to demonstrate how it can be applied in assessment and intervention with young people who have displayed harmful sexual behaviour. Specific techniques from narrative therapy will also be discussed and how these ideas can be used to assist young people to develop safer, more respectful lives.

During the past 20 years there have been considerable developments in the understanding of, and approaches to, working with children and young people who have engaged in harmful sexual behaviour, with strengths-based approaches proving the most effective. The theoretical framework described here is underpinned by the solution-focused practice of de Shazer (1988) and the narrative therapy of White and Epston (1990). Practitioners of both approaches have engaged with children and young people and their families using this approach, which encourages responsibility-taking for the behaviour and for future safety, but without viewing the harmful sexual behaviour as an intrinsic part of the person. Practitioners equally recognise that any harmful behaviour is not to be minimised, and they are mindful of actual and potential victim safety from the outset.

See the person as being more than their problem/difficulty

Harmful sexual behaviour falls within the arena of child protection. It is within this context that a constructive relationship between practitioner and family is crucial, although the very strong feelings associated with the behaviour can make it one of the most difficult times to forge a productive alliance. Where a parent is concerned about the safety of others, often their other children, it is very easy for the work to become dominated by the problems and risks. This over-emphasis on the concerns reduces the likelihood of identifying safer practices already evident within the family system. This in turn can impact on the partnerships that can be built between the practitioner and family.

Turnell and Edwards (1999) outline the key ingredients in forging working relationships that have a shared meaning and goal:

- Parents and children want to be cared about as individuals and to have their strengths acknowledged as well as their weaknesses disclosed.

- They want to know that their story and their perspective regarding the allegations or incidents have been heard and understood.

- It makes a significant difference to families if the worker is responsive and sensitive to the turmoil and stress that the child protection process places on the family.

- The practitioner/agency should be explicit with the family regarding what it expects from them, rather than just focusing on what they have done wrong.

- The family wants to be listened to regarding their wishes and ideas they have to improve the situation.

(adapted from Turnell and Edwards 1999, p.34)

Research into the relationships between families involved in child protection services in Minnesota and their care workers (Skrypek, Idzelis and Pecora 2012) provided an insight into what constitutes a positive working relationship between the family and the worker and was key to successful outcomes. These include a relationship in which workers withhold judgement, demonstrate respect, genuinely listen, are honest and straightforward, and express concerns for the family's wellbeing. Crucially, this meant that families felt they had a clear understanding of what needed to change and how to go about making these changes.

The solution-focused approach also emphasises people's resources and resilience and considers how these can be used in the pursuit of purposeful, positive change. As such the process of increasing levels of safety and ways in which the family is going to achieve this is co-constructed between the practitioner and the family.

Looking for resources rather than deficits

Solution-focused assessments are approached from the belief that young people and their families have strengths, resources and abilities which can be utilised in providing a way forward for the purpose of increasing future safety. Searching for these strengths is not always straightforward and there is at times a requirement for some rigorous and respectful persistence on the part of the worker. Wheeler (2005) likens this process to 'panning for gold'; opportunities can emerge with perseverance and it is essential to locate and build upon the smallest sign of safety when developing a life that is free of the sexually problematic behaviour.

CASE EXAMPLE: WILLIAM (PART 1)

William is a 15-year-old who is sexually attracted to young boys. Other than declaring his love for a younger boy at his school and becoming depressed at the subsequent rejection, his sexually concerning behaviour has to date been limited to following young children into public toilets. He took no personal responsibility for not going further with these young boys, explaining that his school friends had prevented his behaviour from escalating. The following is an excerpt from a transcript of the first session of the work.

Judith: Has there been a time you could have abused a young child and you didn't?

William: Once.

Judith: Yeah, could you tell me about that? This is important.

William: OK.

Judith: Because you can't help the feelings you have but you can take responsibility for the behaviour. You know…feelings of…

William: It's quite strange really. Me and a friend were babysitting for three younger boys. This is incredible really, and I'm there thinking, but I don't really, seriously ever contemplate abusing them or anything like that. It's just too far down the hard road for me, it's…when I was younger, I used to think, I'd done something wrong. It's when you're caught that's fine, when you're caught and you're punished. That's all right. It's just the bit beforehand, you know, when you're waiting to get caught that's the worst bit. That's the bit I can't deal with but, anyway, this, I don't think this boy, there was this one boy in particular, you see, that I liked and I don't think, these boys were prepared very well. Well one of them [inaudible] That's why me and my friend were babysitting. And her dad was dying in hospital and one day she went out visiting her dad and her car had been stolen and her husband had just left her, and things piled up like that. And one night I was putting the boy to bed and he just came out, he asked me to do something sexual to him. And now, my friend was in the other room but somehow, that could have been the reason why I didn't, but also I'd built up an emotional attachment to the nice boy 'cos I'd seen him for a couple of weeks and, I just didn't. For some reason, you know, I'd been waiting for this chance for a long time, and for some reason I didn't want to, I didn't do it. I felt bad about it, I felt guilty. And, you know, I told him [inaudible] I said you shouldn't, don't do that, it's not right. It's not the right thing to do.

Judith: How did you do that? You know, you had been waiting for this chance for a long time, how did you do it?

William: It wasn't like an incredible act of will or anything like that, it wasn't like hard. It was simply like that split second, I regretted it afterwards, even you know, that split second I was just a totally normal person. I didn't want to, you know, 'cos I'd built up this, when I got this special…those sort of feelings were lessened towards that particular boy. It's no problem towards other boys and it's as though that's normal or something, it's quite different.

Strengths that are especially useful in developing safety can be personal qualities such as developing a sense of responsibility-taking, even in a rudimentary form as in the example of William previously. Strengths can also include showing respectful behaviours, demonstrating skills and values that encourage friendships, strengthening and feeling a sense of belonging to family and social networks or pursuing new interests and engaging in education and training. Such 'social anchors' have been identified as central in preventing further harmful behaviour (Chaffin 2008). Thus it is important to address both the harmful sexual behaviour and also wider family and environmental issues when supporting a young person in keeping safe from further sexually concerning behaviour. This is a principle which underpins our work and we have found it effective in engagement and outcomes, even with the most concerning of cases. When we locate strengths they then need to be considered within the context of how they can be applied to contributing to increasing future safety; all our conversations are underpinned by the notion of increasing safety. Strengths in themselves do not equate to safety; it is how they are used to build safety.

Exploring possible and preferred safe futures

The practice principles which underpin the work provide a framework where the safety of everyone is consistently reviewed and remains the focus of the work. There is an expectation that the young person will take responsibility for their behaviour and future safety.

Turnell and Edwards (1999) report that it is much more productive when working towards creating change to help the family to *start* doing something in contrast to getting someone to *stop* doing something. This doesn't condone any abusive behaviour that has occurred but highlights to the family that they have the experience and knowledge which can be built upon for the purpose of increasing safety. Where harmful sexual behaviour has occurred between siblings, families are asked what else they intend to do differently to increase levels of safety within the home. Often families have already begun to put in place safety measures, such as staggered bedtimes, changed sleeping arrangements and have adopted stricter rules about playing in bedrooms and getting dressed in bedrooms/bathrooms. It is helpful if the worker lists these family safety rules in chart form so that they can either be displayed in the home or kept in bedrooms (see Figure 2.1 on page 39).

CASE EXAMPLE

Blake is an 11-year-old boy who had put his finger on his five-year-old sister's vulva whilst in the bath. Blake disclosed that he had got the idea from watching a late night movie on his television, which was in his bedroom. The safe care plan was structured with the whole family during the assessment process.

 PRACTICE ACTIVITY

Consider a family you are working with and complete a safe care plan with them, using Figure 2.2 on page 40.

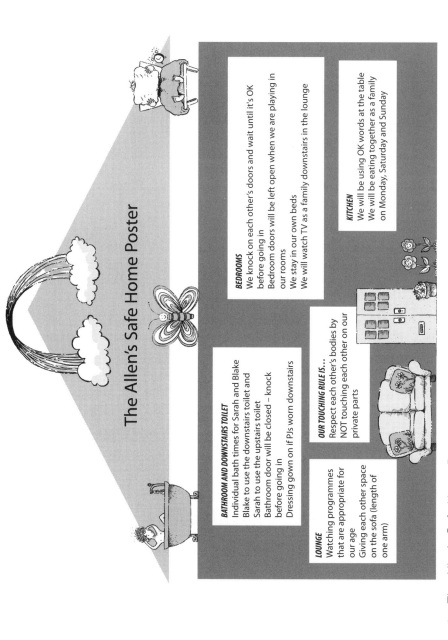

Figure 2.1 The Allen's Safe Home Poster

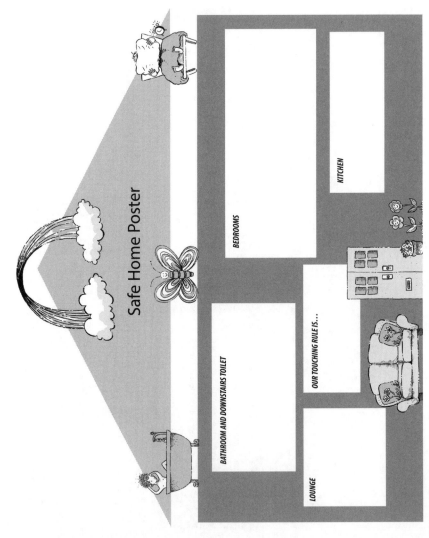

Figure 2.2 Safe Home Poster

Identifying what is already happening that is working towards those safe futures

> Search for exceptions to the problem. This creates hope for workers and families by proving that the problem does not always exist. Exceptions may also indicate solutions that have worked in the past. Where no exceptions exist, the worker may be alerted to a more serious problem. (Turnell and Edwards 1999, p.51)

An important principle of solution-focused work is the recognition that there will usually be exceptions to the concerning behaviour. Enquiring about these times is based on the belief that the worrying behaviour is not a constant presence and there will be times when the person is behaving appropriately. Inevitably any such behaviour would warrant some form of professional intervention but within the process it would also be helpful to ensure that equal weight is given to finding out what is going well in the person's life and the presence of safe and appropriate behaviour.

When considering exceptions a worker will rigorously look and enquire explicitly about those times when the young person has demonstrated safer, more respectful behaviour. There will also be a focus on times when the young person may have been presented with opportunities to behave inappropriately but didn't do so. There will be a search about what was different on these occasions, asking 'when', 'where', 'how' and 'what' questions. Such enquiry can begin to give an appreciation not only of the young person's values and internal boundaries but also an insight into the values of wider family members and the rules that govern the house. Obviously this doesn't always result in a gathering of evidence that warrants an assessment of increased safety; equally, it can provide information that gives cause for concern. Exception-finding questions include:

- Can you tell me about times when you have demonstrated safe sexual behaviour/respectful behaviour?

- Can you tell me about times when s/he has demonstrated safe sexual behaviour/respectful behaviour?

- What did this look like? If I was looking through the window and observed you being safe and respectful to your sister what would that look like?

- Who else would know this about you?
- Were there times when the behaviour could have shown itself and didn't?
- What was different?
- How did you manage to do this? What steps did you take?
- What needs to happen so that more of this occurs?
- Can you tell me about a time when the problem wasn't around?

CASE EXAMPLE: WILLIAM (PART 2)

William could describe only one time when he was able to resist an opportunity for sexual contact with a young boy but this can be developed into stronger resistance to the expression of his sexual feelings by asking questions about his notions of 'right care', something for which he will be able to take personal responsibility and build into his future way of being.

Judith: That was quite a big thing you did there. A sort of foolproof situation for you, wasn't it? And yet you resisted it…was it hard or was it easy?

William: It was easy to resist. I think it is because there were facts against me, you know, the fact that I wasn't alone with the boy in the house. And the fact that I wouldn't be able to live with the waiting to be found out afterwards, I don't think. So there were those sort of… I suppose, but then there was that, for one moment I saw that right care [indistinguishable] if you've got that option towards them again I don't think, it was still at a time when I was accepting the feelings but I thought they were wrong still. Whereas now, it's quite easy to go down the road where I convince myself they're all right. You think it's a society thing more, the human thing, it's the fashion for society at the moment for paedophilia to be wrong. Even today, in some very distant cultures, like Papua New Guinea, there are practices where they still do that. And in Ancient Greece, they used to as well. And is it only a matter of time, if we span a cycle on of 2000 years, will paedophilia be rife and legal and accepted again? I think it's a fashion trend of society. It's easy to convince myself. I forget, you know, I know it's wrong at the moment. Serious jail… I forget… Judith: So, we can look at the bigger issues but the fact remains that in our society it's wrong. So what do you think is right care for young people?

William went on to develop his thinking into right and wrong love, over which he had little control, and right and wrong care, which he could do, and did, something about.

Respecting children and their families' knowledge and meanings

There is a plethora of government guidance recommending effective practice and what this looks like when working with children and families. Core skills such as communication and listening are often a feature of these documents. Unfortunately, what often appears to be missed is discussion of the process which follows talking and listening to families, which is the interpretation of what has been said. Dalrymple and Burke (1995) suggest that professionals are not unwilling to talk with and listen to families but that answers are interpreted within a professional frame of reference. Solution-focused practice is interested in hearing the individual's perspective and explanation of their situation, with an emphasis on how this is managed and a way forward. Thompson (2003) argues the importance of effective listening if we are to be successful in our attempts to communicate, so we:

- Note idiosyncratic use of language, repeated words, language that sticks out, for example, William's use of the words 'right care'.

- Enquire about any word or phrase that appears to have special meaning for the young person.

- Check with the young person that we have the same meaning of the word and/or picture used. This is especially important when they have picked up formal language from professionals, such as 'appropriate behaviour' or words for parts of the body. We have found it is not uncommon for young people to use the word 'vagina' when they mean 'vulva'.

- Take care not to edit young people's words in our reports, and make sure that our conversations develop from the young person's words, not our own.

- Only ask questions to which we do not think we know the answer so that we are not jumping to conclusions and making assumptions.

- Listen to the reply to one question before deciding what our next question is going to be.

- Ask the young person if we are asking questions that are interesting/relevant to them.

- Ask the young person if there are any questions we haven't asked that are important to them (Milner and Bateman 2011).

Respecting and acknowledging people's knowledge and meaning is an important aspect of building cooperative relationships. This in no way means that any abusive behaviour is being condoned but enables important information to be gathered about both concerns and safety, and puts the worker side-by-side with the family in the process of facilitating change, a constructive relationship being the key to successful outcomes.

This is developed further with the belief, integral to this way of working, that each person is the 'expert' in their own life and is equipped with the knowledge of what works best for them, even though their expertise may have been undermined by the structural inequalities which affect many service users' lives. The individual's expertise is continuously validated in conversations, so that they can find a way to take responsibility for their behaviour, and begin to locate solutions and a way forward.

The expertise of a solution-focused practitioner is in holding conversations and being curious about a way forward to enable children and their families to locate their knowledge, strengths, skills and abilities which will support them in this journey. The attention to detail and providing context to families' resources, particularly when considering safety, is also vital. For example, whilst gathering information on strengths and abilities provides a level of awareness and a foundation for the family to build upon, where previously this may have been neglected and/or unnoticed, it is equally important to enquire about their understanding of how they can then *apply* this to increased levels of safety within the family home.

✏️ **PRACTICE ACTIVITY**

The next time you are talking to a young person with whom you are working, ask them about their good qualities, what this says about them as a person, and how can they use these qualities to help solve their problem.

Some young people have met so much negativity that they find this sort of conversation difficult, so plan how you will help your young person identify and amplify their good qualities, however small.

Externalising

The narrative approach of Michael White and David Epston (1990) also focuses on individual strengths, exceptions and future functioning. But more than solution-focused practice, the narrative approach gives more weight to the presence and influence of power and is also concerned with the 'dominant' understandings and narratives that have the power to impact oppressively on a person's understanding of themselves and their lives. This latter issue is very visible within this area of work, with descriptions such as 'paedophile' and 'perpetrator' being easily and comfortably shared between professionals. These dominant descriptions can result in 'truths' being generated about a person's identity which can be restrictive, can generate assumptions about a person's actions and rationale for their behaviour, and can lead to inaccurate risk assessments.

✎ **PRACTICE ACTIVITY**

- What words are used in your agency to describe young people whose behaviour is sexually concerning or harmful?

- What impact do you think these words have on the young people to whom they are applied?

- Are there other words you could use that are accurate but less stigmatising?

Problem-saturated narratives can become deeply entrenched in an individual's sense of self, impacting upon how a person perceives their own identity, and how they are perceived by others. This is particularly relevant when considering the highly emotive subject of sexually concerning and harmful behaviour. A problem-saturated story limits perspective and edits out alternative narratives which contradict the problem, making change seem unlikely (Freeman, Epston and Lobovits 1997, p.48). The impact of this is that possibilities around increasing future safety can be limited.

An important technique of narrative practice is that of externalisation, the intention being to separate the person from the problem to create space between the person and the problem:

> Externalisation is an approach...that encourages persons to objectify, and at times personify, the problems that they experience as oppressive. In this process the problem becomes a separate entity and thus external to the person who was, or the relationship that was, ascribed the problem. Those problems that are considered to be inherent, and those relatively fixed qualities that are attributed to persons and to relationships, are rendered less fixed and less restricting. (White 1989, p.1)

Being given the opportunity to view the problem as separate from themselves allows both the young people and their families to put all their efforts into finding a safe solution to the problem rather than being defensive. At the beginning of the work with a young person, 'naming' the sexual behaviour is explored, using language with which the young person feels comfortable. For example, younger children often describe their problem as 'the touching problem'. Older children may choose 'the embarrassing problem' or simply 'it'. Older young people choose more sophisticated descriptions, such as William's 'wrong love'. Young people with learning difficulties may choose a cartoon character to describe their problem, such as 'Mr Just Do It'. The young person's choice of problem description is used by the worker throughout all subsequent conversations. For a fuller explanation of externalising, see Myers *et al.* 2003; Milner 2008.

Externalising problem behaviours enables conversations to be developed around the effects and impact of the behaviour on everyone who was involved and helps to begin a process that leads to finding exceptions to the behaviour, times when the behaviour didn't happen. The worker can ask challenging questions when they are addressing the problem rather than the person. Such questions include:

- What effect or influence does the touching problem have on your life, on those people who are important to you, on these relationships, on how you think about yourself?
- What influence or impact do you have on the touching problem?
- Would you prefer life with the touching problem or life free of the touching problem?
- When did the touching problem move into your life?
- What does this say about what you want for your (and others') life and what is important to you for you to make this stand? What will be the first steps you take in achieving this?

These conversations begin to provide greater understanding of the young person's position: whether or not they believe the behaviour was appropriate, how this fits with their view of themselves as a person, and how they want to be viewed by the important people in their lives and society. It also helps the worker make an accurate assessment of how willing the young person is to take responsibility for creating safety. Where this willingness is absent, external safety constraints will be required.

Narrative letters

Epston and White developed narrative letters as a way of providing continuous feedback on sessions (White and Epston 1990; Epston 1998). Letter writing not only documents and provides a frame of reference to conversations already had but continues and extends conversations after the session has ended. For example, when a young person has spoken of their ability to behave in a more sexually respectful way, thus demonstrating exceptions to the problem, a narrative letter will recognise and amplify those occasions which are consistent with their preferred identity. Using the person's own words, a narrative letter provides a check on the worker's perceptions, reduces power imbalances, encourages co-authorship and enables the worker to ask further questions as well as documenting progress.

CASE EXAMPLE

Tom is a 17-year-old who was made the subject of a three-year supervision order. There had been longstanding concerns about Tom displaying sexually concerning behaviour. When the referral was made there had been a number of complaints from females within the community of Tom attempting to smell and touch their feet.

Hello Tom

Here are our notes from when we met on 12 July.

You are still doing some cooking for yourself. You have been doing this with your dad and by yourself. You feel more motivated to do this as you are not 'stoned' any more. Benjamin has noticed this and has been giving you credit for this. Sarah has also commented on your new skills. Your dad is going on holiday soon, so you are going to try to cook more for yourself. You think this is a good idea and feel OK about this new responsibility and increased independence. I was wondering how this increased responsibility and independence could be helpful to you within other areas of your life. In fact, it may be already having a presence in other ways. Maybe you could take time to spot these occasions and let me know when we next meet.

Thinking about the presence of cannabis, you have continued to take steps in trying to keep it out of your life. In fact, since I last saw you on 3 June you have smoked on two occasions where previously you told me that you smoked every day. These two recent times were on days when you say you were feeling stressed. At the same time there have been other stressful days when you have not smoked cannabis and you have used the ideas that you identified in your session on 3 June.

You have found kicking cannabis out of your life difficult, particularly at the beginning. After a week you 'felt a lot better about myself', were 'more motivated', 'waking up feeling refreshed instead of rough'. Your mates have noticed and they were taking the piss for a little while but have now stopped. You have not told them the real reason for kicking out cannabis. This is private to you. Your dad has noticed as he said, 'I know you've stopped smoking as you are not coming in with your eyes shut.' You say your dad thinks you have two personalities when cannabis is around. When you're not stoned you are giddy, and lifeless when you are. You prefer to be giddy.

You spoke of your recognition that 'the touching' is greater in size when you are stoned as you feel less in control and more likely to go up to someone. You said that being stoned was not helpful to you. We spoke some more about your relationship with cannabis and although cannabis doesn't affect your relationship with mates you identified that it did with your parents. You don't think that you will find it hard to keep cannabis out of your life and feel able to say no to your mates if they offer you any.

It was recognised in your session that over time you have experienced different levels of control of 'the touching' but saying that 'the touching' has remained absent from your life for a significant period of time now. It was recognised that there may be times when you are a little less in control but that you are aware of these times and what would be helpful to ensure that 'the touching' doesn't show itself. Tom, you are aware of when you are not in control as you start to think a lot about people's feet. This, however, has never happened since you were in trouble. You have stopped yourself by thinking about those two days in a cell and going to court. You say this has always been enough.

Tom, we spoke about your work coming to an end. You feel OK about this but 'still feel that I need a bit of help'. When we considered what this help could look like you mentioned 'just being able to talk about it'. It was recognised that you can talk to Claire at those times. It was also agreed that if you wanted to come for a chat that you could ring up and we would arrange a time.

I hope all this is correct.

See you on 2 August.

Jackie

As highlighted in the previous case example, these letters can enable conversations from sessions to be extended and bridge the gap between sessions. Letters can be extensions to the conversations already shared in sessions. They will typically enquire how the young person is going to continue their quest in developing safety. Furthermore, as sessions typically include family/carers they may ask these significant others to continue to notice these and other occasions which contradict the problem narrative, which will support the young person on their journey.

CASE EXAMPLE

Benjamin is 25 years old and the elder brother of Tom. At the beginning of the work their relationship was quite fractious. Benjamin was embarrassed by his younger brother's behaviour, which resulted in them either ignoring each other or having arguments. However, there had been some noticeable improvements after a recent home visit which led to the following letter.

Dear Benjamin

I hope you are well. I am writing to you in connection with the conversation we had a few weeks ago about you contributing some thoughts about the changes you have noticed with Tom. I hope this is still OK. Your thoughts could be shared at the next meeting.

Tom has spoken about your relationship and how things have improved. I am aware through our conversation that you share a similar feeling.

During our work together particular strengths have been identified which appear to have been a striking force in supporting Tom to take control of 'the touching' as well as identified by Tom as strengths which are important to him. These strengths are determination, responsibility and independence, not being scared to do things, caring and coping.

I would be interested to hear of other stories or knowledge you have of these strengths. I would appreciate your thoughts on the following questions.

- What times/stories can you think of that show these qualities?
- What other strengths, values and qualities have you noticed?
- How long ago did you witness these?
- What does this say to you about Tom?

Any other thoughts would be very welcome. I look forward to hearing from you.

Kind regards,

Jackie

The letters provide an accurate account and reflection of the often courageous conversations that young people have shared in their sessions. Care is taken to include words and statements that have been provided directly by the young person, as well as the general language of the letter being appropriate to the age and development of the young person. Strengths, abilities and skills already present and visible in the young person's life, as well as those that may have been unnoticed and those which are 'work in progress' are documented. There are expressions of curiosity of how this knowledge and resources have contributed to other areas of the young person's life, what impact this has on their identity, what they stand for and how they want to be.

A narrative letter reflects the relationship that the young person has with the problem, whilst at the same time ensuring that the problem is spoken of in a way that separates them from the problem. The content celebrates the positive events, as well as giving recognition to the struggles and pain that a young person may disclose. What is particularly important to hold in mind when undertaking any such writings is that these are accounts which are defined by the young person and/or family and are not edited by the worker.

Within this writing process, we are mindful that equal attention is given to any unsafe behaviour by the young person.

✎ PRACTICE ACTIVITY

- Ask a young person if it is OK with them for you to take notes. Write down as much of what the young person says about their progress as possible. This means that you will have to ask the young person to slow down, repeat some sentences and check that you have written things down correctly. This will provide the person with space in which to reflect on what they are saying. It will also prevent you from talking too much.

- Construct a letter from your notes and send it to the young person. Where the young person has a learning disability, charts, pictures, maps and stories are used. These are discussed more fully in Chapter 6.

Constructing a narrative letter is time consuming, especially when you have to write a further account for agency records. In these circumstances the letter and agency recording can be combined using the format outlined by Berg and Reuss (1998, p.167) in their work with mandated alcohol misusers.

CASE EXAMPLE

Session notes
Name: Dwayne
Date: 23 April

Problem

Dwayne, 14, has a touching problem. He touched his sister, Crystal, on her private parts and when he was sent to live with his dad, he did the same with Kayden. His mum also says that he is disrespectful to her and Crystal (although Crystal can be just as bad at times). Mum is especially upset about Dwayne's touching because her mum was sexually abused by her dad and ended up in care.

Mum would like Dwayne to be more respectful and all her children to be safe. Crystal doesn't want him to touch her again. Dwayne would like to find an easier way of living – at the moment he doesn't feel at all good about himself (he's only at 10 out of a 100 on the 'feeling good about himself' scale).

Progress

1. Everyone is lot safer now and Dwayne is very sorry about what he did.

2. Dwayne can do respect a bit. He reckons he is at 3 on the respect scale and his mum would put him at 2 or 3 (out of 10).

3. He is at 3 or 4 on the responsibility-taking scale (out of 10). Mum agrees with this.

4. He is also a bit truthful – about 20 per cent of the time.

Solutions

1. At first, Dwayne thought that Crystal didn't mind what he did because she put her hands down his trousers and her fingers through his hair but she told about it at school so he knows she didn't like it. Everyone is safer because Dwayne is sleeping on the top floor and has his own bathroom. The bathrooms all have locks and the family is respecting privacy more. Before, they used to go around half naked. Dwayne doesn't go into the girls' rooms except to take their clean washing in.

2. Dwayne is respectful with his sister Kiera. Judith saw him being kind and helpful with her over her breakfast. He also knows how to be respectful with Ben, the dog. He plays with Ben nicely and takes care of him. He respects his friends too. They all like him and he listens to them and helps them with their problems. Mum says Dwayne is funny, intelligent, good looking and can be very good. If he was being more respectful to her he would be telling the truth more, helping around the house more, listening and keeping out of trouble.

3. Dwayne only does responsibility-taking when there is something in it for him. But then he does it well, like sharing mum's catalogue delivery work with her. Mum is going to take £15 a week from his earnings so that he can learn more about responsibility-taking.

4. Judith forgot to ask Dwayne how he does truthfulness.

Homework

1. To make a start on building respect and finding an easier way of living, Dwayne will do enough respect to please mum as keeping his bathroom clean would do. Or maybe both!

2. Judith will do some keep safe work with Crystal.

Date of next appointment: 4 May

✎ **PRACTICE ACTIVITY**

Think about how you could adapt your agency's recording practices to provide narrative written feedback.

Summary

It is easier to measure safety than risk. An over-emphasis on locating risk limits the possibilities of identifying safer practices, which in turn can impact adversely on the relationship between the worker and family. Strengths-based assessments give serious consideration to individual and family resources, skills and abilities, specifically how they influence and contribute towards increasing levels of safety but without minimising the concerning behaviour. It is more beneficial when increasing levels of safety to help the family to start doing something than to stop them doing something.

Externalising conversations provide a forum for the person to discuss their relationship with the harmful sexual behaviour. The technique provides adequate distance which neither sees the behaviour as intrinsic to the individual nor takes responsibility away for the behaviour.

CHAPTER 3

Assessing Risk and Building Safety

This chapter explains how to undertake risk assessments and develop safety plans using a Signs of Safety framework. Detailed case examples are provided.

Most assessment models used in responding to sexual offending are problem focused in that the focus is firmly on the sexual offending behaviour thus the identification of risk is not only given priority but is also located within the individual and their networks (see, for example, the 'cycle of abuse', G-map outlined in Morrison, Erooga and Beckett 1994). The person whose behaviour is sexually offensive is viewed as suffering from a pathological disorder for which a diagnosis is required before a cure can be prescribed. This subsequently leads to the idea that an expert is required who is equipped to find out what is wrong and fix the problem. However, when there is this preoccupation with risk, practice can become rigid and fixated towards simply finding, assessing and/or hypothesising potential risk, especially when deciding whether the risk is high, medium or low. This isn't very helpful as most people fall into a medium risk level and, in any case, low risk behaviours can still happen. When young people's behaviour is interpreted in this way, they can become subject to a discourse of deviancy (Cossins 2000) restricting possibilities of change, evoking instead positions of shame and blame. Furthermore, applying pathologising discourses runs the risk of distancing the young person from developing a preferred safer, respectful identity. As young people grow and develop they are constantly negotiating and constructing their identities, so classifying young people as 'mini' paedophiles or perpetrators restricts this development and ignores the social context of their lives. When there is an over-reliance on reducing risk opportunities, looking for evidence of safety and safe sexual practice can be lost. The 2013 Criminal Justice Joint Inspection found that 'most of the work to address offending behaviour was not delivered as identified in various plans, and interventions were not always informed by assessments' (p. 7). We outline how a holistic Signs of Safety model maintains a rigorous focus on the seriousness of the problems and concerns but also is fundamentally organised around future safety (Turnell and Essex 2006, p.11).

Assessing safety

An assessment which is underpinned by solution-focused and narrative practice principles (de Shazer 1988; White and Epston 1990) provides an alternative framework in the assessment and intervention of young people who display harmful sexual behaviour. Strengths-based models of assessment are recommended in *Working Together 2010* (5.5) and have been found to produce better outcomes for children and young people (DCSF, 2010), and in October 2014, a £4.7 million grant was awarded to Munro, Turnell & Murphy Child Protection Consulting to fully implement the Signs of Safety model in ten local authorities in England[1]. The aim of the assessment is to determine the level of intervention required to assist the young person in maintaining a future that is free of sexually problematic behaviour. To this end the following goals have been developed by Barnardo's The Junction, a specialist service for children and young people with sexually concerning or harmful behaviour:

- To be specific about the detail of the alleged sexually concerning behaviour

- To clarify what everyone understands about the behaviour and their individual levels of concern (child/young person, family, victim, and agency)

- To consider how the behaviour has already been responded to

---

1   See the Signs of Safety website, www.signsofsafety.net/signs-of-safety-england-innovations-project, for more information on the UK implementation of the model.

- To identify what works in assisting the child/young person to avoid the sexually concerning behaviour

- To agree a strategy for maintaining a problem-free future and to develop safety

- To establish the motivation and ability of participants to work towards safety (Myers and Milner 2007, p.155).

✎ **PRACTICE ACTIVITY**

Think about a young person with whom you are not making much progress. Examine your goals for the work and then ask yourself if you need to add any of the goals listed previously. If so, how will you go about discussing them with the young person?

Establishing achievable, measurable and ethical goals is essential. Professional goals should set a foundation to the work and provide clarity so the young person, family and relevant organisations are aware of what the expectations are, what needs to be demonstrated and within what timescales. From a children's social care perspective this is what needs to happen for workers to be confident that levels of safety are sufficient for the case to be closed. From a teacher's or youth worker's perspective it is what needs to happen to ensure that other children and young people in their care are safe. Within this overarching safety goal there is room for the family and the young person's personal goals to be met. Very often, the most immediate family one is avoiding having to move because of the shame and possible adverse reactions from neighbours. The young person's goal is often, for example, simply to be allowed back to football club. Useful questions to explore family goals include:

- What needs to happen for you to know that the work has been useful?

- What would you like to see happen as a result of us working together?

When a response is 'for there to be no professionals in our lives', although it is important to recognise this is an understandable response, supplementary questions are asked to place responsibility back on the family members:

- OK, what needs to happen before professionals are happy not to be in your life?
- What do you need to do to contribute to this process?
- What do professionals need to see demonstrated so that they can close the case?

Setting clear goals at the beginning of the work is crucial to the assessment process, and remaining focused on them increases the likelihood of positive outcomes. Quite simply you can ask the young person and their family what are their best hopes. Another way of obtaining a detailed goal is to ask a 'miracle question' as devised by de Shazer (1988), a solution-focused technique which has successfully engaged young people and their families in the development of concrete goals. There are various versions of the question which can be tailored to the context of the work; for example, some children whose behaviour is sexually concerning have themselves been sexually assaulted from an early age and may associate the word 'miracle' or 'magic' with ways in which they were made to keep the abuse secret, especially as the question involves bedtime and sleep. We would pose the question something like this: *Suppose that after we have finished talking today, you do all the things you usually do in the day and then you go to bed and have a really sound sleep. No bad dreams, nothing but peaceful sleep, but while you are asleep something wonderful happens and all the things that got you into this trouble have gone. But, because you were fast asleep, you don't at first know this.*

Having set the scenario, you then follow up with a series of detailed questions. We offer some specimen questions below but each question needs to follow each answer closely with the intention of discovering the minute details of what this particular person's solution will look like:

- *What will be the first thing that is different that will tell you that this has happened?*

- *What will you notice?*

- *What will your mum, dad, friends notice?*

- *How would I know things have changed?*

- *What difference will there be in your relationship with your mum, dad, sister, brother?*

- *What will be different at school? What will your teachers notice?*

Discussing what will be happening in the absence of the harmful sexual behaviour provides the young person with opportunities to consider the details of what life could look like when the unwanted behaviour is no longer present. This opens up conversations around goals and hopes. In addition to this, supplementary questions could be asked which identify times, events and circumstances when this detail has actually taken place and how, what and when this happened – the exceptions you will use to build safety. When we record these details we separate what happened (the progress) from how it happened (the solutions) so that the young person knows exactly what they did right and how they did it so they can then do more of it.

CASE EXAMPLE

Session notes
Name: Keiron
Date: 5 October

Problem
Keiron, 15, has two problems: *saying sexy things to his brothers* (and sometimes other lads and lasses), and *doing sexy things to his brother* Lewis, 12. He wants to get more control over these problems so that there will be less danger and more safety without mum having to keep an eye on him or remind him all the time.

When Keiron has more control over the problems, he will be able to socialise more because mum won't be worried about there being no one to supervise him. Keiron is a pretty happy person but he would like to be a better person. At the moment he rates himself at about 40–45 per cent and he'd rather be at 80–90 per cent.

Progress

1. Keiron has got to 5+ on the *controlling saying sexy things* scale where 1 is *Keiron would say sexy things every time he got a chance* and 10 is *he would never say them.*

2. He has got to 5 on the controlling doing sexy things scale where 1 is *Keiron would do sexy things every time he got the chance* and 10 is *he never would.*

3. Before, he used to skip school and argue with mum about homework and her restrictions but now he's OK about it all. He's attending school and concentrating in his lessons.

4. Although sometimes Keiron doesn't take any notice of when Lewis says no, he always does with lasses.

5. Keiron is pretty happy because he's making progress and knows the good things about himself.

Solutions

1. Keiron got up to 5+ on the *controlling saying sexy things* scale by taking notice when Lewis says 'shut up'. Most times he can handle it and not repeat it again. He's been doing this for quite a long time and feels proud of himself for it.

2. He got to 5 on the *controlling doing sexy things* scale by thinking it over and controlling it for that moment. Distraction helps but mainly he has thought what it could do to his life. Talking about risks to himself as well as others has helped.

3. Keiron is OK about the restrictions because he knows they are for his safety as well as others'. He's going to school and doing his homework because he thinks he's got a future. He intends to work hard at school so that he can be a plumber.

4. Keiron takes notice when lasses say no because he thinks about how they feel. Sometimes this is easy, sometimes it's hard but he hasn't taken it too far with any lass.

5. Keiron says the good things about himself are: he's sporty, strong, good at school, good at helping round the house, able to relax and handsome (he can get loads of lasses). Mum says he's kind (always brings her a cup of tea in the morning), responsible (remembers to take his dog out), helps granddad with things, and has just become good at having

a joke with people. So, there's quite a lot of respectfulness and responsibility-taking that will come in useful for solving Keiron's problems.

Next steps

Stopping doing sexy things is the most important part of the problem for Keiron so he will do more things to take his mind off it. As well, he will make a start on thinking about a *keeping safe plan* (safe for himself and Lewis). One of mum's big worries is what would happen if Lewis got to the bus station in the morning before Keiron had got on his bus, so this is where Keiron will start his safety plan. He can use his kindness and thoughtfulness to help him. And being more grown up.

Name of practitioner: Judith
Date and time of next appointment: 19 October at 10.30 a.m.

Being specific about the detail of the alleged sexually concerning behaviour

Within any assessment it is important to gather sufficient quality information that will provide depth and context to the situation that is being assessed. In beginning to assess the seriousness of any sexually concerning behaviour, we discuss with the young person the following aspects of the behaviour:

- *Distress caused by the behaviour, specifically to the victim but also any witnesses and family members.* As we saw in the case example of Dwayne (see Chapter 2), he had underestimated the upset he caused his sister and was completely unaware of his mum's feelings.

- *The type of behaviour, the degree of intrusion and/or adult-like behaviour.* Not surprisingly, most young people minimise the seriousness of their behaviour – as many people who are responsible for a minor bump in their car do when they report to their insurers – but it is important to make it clear to the young person what sorts of behaviours could result in a custodial sentence and/or a schedule 1 offender record and the impact this would have on their future.

- *Any power differences between the victim and the person who displayed the behaviour by virtue of age, intelligence, size, status.* This is not always straightforward. Keiron, for example, was considerably older and bigger than Lewis but Lewis was more intelligent and adept at winding up his brother.

- *The degree of any coercion, threats or force used.* This isn't always about physical force; many young people just aren't aware of the power of their threats and persuasion. For example, 16-year-old Stuart had seemed to understand that his younger brother and sister were easily led by him and that he could not be allowed unsupervised contact with them until he helped with safety work aimed at enabling the young children to say no to him in a range of situations. Frustrated at the slowness of the pace of the work, he threatened his sister with 'Get on with the work because otherwise I won't be allowed to come and play with you.' Needless to say, the safety work was suspended and work with Stuart on power in family relationships was rethought.

- *The number of times the behaviour is displayed, listing this as historic, recent and current to aid the focus of the work.* For example, a list of the number of times 15-year-old Jerome's sexual behaviour was problematic gives the impression of a hardened serial offender:

  1. Jerome played willy games as a young child.
  2. He sexually assaulted a seven-year-old boy.
  3. He is alleged to have had penetrative sex with a 12-year-old boy.
  4. He touched a vulnerable girl inappropriately.
  5. He can be dominating.

  However, points 1 and 2 are historic (and he was seven when the assault took place), point 3 is recent (albeit denied), whereas points 4 and 5 are current and provide an appropriate starting point for the work.

- *Where the behaviour happened.* Listing where Jerome's sexually problematic behaviour occurred adds useful context. The first two events occurred in his own home, the seven-year-old being the son of one of his mother's partners. The third event is alleged to have happened on a visit to another of his mother's partners. The fourth occurred on the way home from school and the fifth – his dominating behaviour – is confined to his relationship with his mother for whom he is a carer due to her longstanding mental ill health.

- *Whether any consent was given and the validity of this consent.* Jerome thought it OK to touch the girl inappropriately because she had been willing. However, she had mild learning difficulties so her ability to give informed consent was doubtful.

- *The frequency and duration of time over which any sexually concerning behaviour has been occurring* as, usually, the longer established the behaviour is the more difficult it is for the young person to resist temptation.

PRACTICE ACTIVITY

Bearing in mind that it not possible to have a constructive conversation with a young person when the topics are all negative, think about how you would begin to talk with Jerome about his behaviour.

This information begins to provide a context to the harmful sexual behaviour, although it would be counterproductive to spend a session entirely on these details. Equally it is important to gather details about the strengths, skills, resources and goals of the young person and family, and exceptions to the harmful sexual behaviour. Eliciting detailed information about both concerns and safety, drawn from all domains of a family's life, provides a safety net for the practitioner from being either overly optimistic or overly negative as the assessment is both holistic and evidence based.

During this process assumptions are not made without clear evidence. Within the arena of sexual offending, pathologising discourses are often privileged, which can result in an over-estimation of the danger that a young person's behaviour may pose. Equally, there can be a minimisation of the behaviour and its impact, where the behaviour is deemed exploratory and normalised, and as such leads to an under-estimation of the seriousness of what has happened. As one mother is quoted in The Junction's Safe Care guide for parents:

> I needed back up for myself. My sister thought it was just kids growing up. We had different views on the problem. I was beside myself. I couldn't sleep, couldn't think about anything else, couldn't even tidy a room. The worker backing me up helped. And telling me it was a problem, but it was minor. (Barnardo's 2005, p.3)

To safeguard against either of these outcomes it is recommended that professionals use language that reflects an accurate description of the behaviour that was displayed and the context of this. For example, Jerome described his 'inappropriate touching' as putting his finger in the girl's vagina but further discussion revealed his lack of knowledge of anatomical language, he had actually stroked her vulva – a much less serious offence in legal terms as no penetration had occurred, but just as serious in consent terms.

 PRACTICE ACTIVITY

Make a list of what you think the concerns are in Jerome's case. Taking each concern in turn, list what safety would look like.

Clarify what everyone understands about the behaviour and their individual levels of concern (child/young person, family, victim and agency)

When a young person has displayed harmful sexual behaviour and it comes to the attention of family and/or professionals there can often be a mixture of responses, ranging from shock and anger to concern and alarm. These responses can become combined with uncertainty about the way forward, taking into account the needs of the victim and recognising that it is a young person (and not an adult) who has displayed the behaviour. The young person can become pathologised by both language and by decision making. The young person can also be experiencing feelings of shame, embarrassment and guilt as well as being fearful of the possible consequences of their behaviour. Nevertheless, they often struggle to articulate these thoughts, and professionals can interpret this as minimisation, or lacking empathy or responsibility. This in turn can result in inaccurate assessments about levels of risk that the young person's behaviour may pose. Equally, there can be an assumption that adult family members were aware of or complicit with the behaviour. Even when this clearly isn't the case there can be limited recognition of the trauma that families may be experiencing when such behaviour is unearthed. Parents are often struggling with their own feelings of disgust, shame and guilt and they themselves can become pathologised and vulnerable to social discourses. In light of this it is essential that these emotions are taken into account and not necessarily misinterpreted as parents being reluctant to engage in assessments about their capacity to protect. This doesn't mean that the behaviour is minimised. On the contrary, it is imperative that any initial assessments about level of safety are robust, particularly when the outcome might have a bearing on whether the young person is removed from home.

Below are some questions that begin to elicit a clear understanding of the positions of each family member alongside an acknowledgement that assessments on levels of safety are imperative.

- How has the behaviour changed things for you as a family?
- What have you done differently about keeping everyone safe since you found out about the behaviour?
- What other things are you thinking about that could build upon/contribute to the changes you have already made?
- How have you kept your children safe in the past?
- How have you continued to function as a family since the behaviour came to light?

- How have you coped?
- How serious do you consider the behaviour?
- Whilst respecting your child's position that the behaviour didn't happen how are you going to increase the likelihood of no further allegations being reported?

Specific questions to elicit the young person's understanding of the behaviour and the impact on the victim are also asked:

- What impact has the behaviour had on you, the victim and other family members?
- What impact has the behaviour had on the victim's family?
- How has the behaviour changed your relationship with the victim?
- Do you think the behaviour is OK/not OK?
- How have you come to that decision?
- How concerned are you that the behaviour could show itself again?
- Whilst respecting your position that the behaviour didn't happen how are you going to protect yourself from the likelihood of further allegations being made?

The technique of 'externalising' introduced in Chapter 2 invites the young person to 'name' the concerning behaviour, which then provides some space between them and the problem. This process enables communication to focus specifically on the relationship and position that the young person and family take in relation to the sexually harmfully behaviour (for a detailed example of this in practice, see Myers *et al.* 2003). This in turn creates the potential for the young person to have a richer understanding of their behaviour in contrast to the external construct of the 'cycle of abuse model', where limitations have been identified (Hackett 2000).

Inevitably, there will be situations where the allegations are questioned and/or denied by the young person and their family. It is, however, still possible to create partnerships and for the work to focus on an outcome where no allegations of sexually inappropriate behaviour are made in the future. This will be discussed in greater depth in Chapter 4.

Consider how the behaviour has been responded to previously

> There is no doubt that the child protection worker must gather information about past and potential harm and family deficiencies, but, to balance the picture, it is also vital to obtain information regarding past, existing and potential safety, competencies and strengths. (Turnell and Edwards 1999, p.49)

Young people and their parents can be fearful of the consequences and embarrassed. This can impact on their initial level of engagement in the process and they may not wish to talk about it all: 'I thought, oh my God, everyone's going to know. How is this going to affect him? How is this going to affect me? And at work?' (a mother quoted in the *Safe Care Pack for Parents and Carers*, p.3). In these situations it is helpful to enquire with the family about what is already going well and then specifically how they have responded to the behaviour with the aim of assessing current and future levels of safety.

- What steps have you taken to increase safety since you found out about the behaviour?

- Has this happened before? What did you do that helped? Could you do this again?

- Who is around to support you? How have they helped since the behaviour came to your attention of others?

- What would your daughter need to notice happening in the family for her to feel safer?

- If I asked your son about what would help to make him feel safer, what do you think he would say?

CASE EXAMPLE

When Charlotte discovered that her 14-year-old foster sons Jack and Adam had been in the girls' bedroom (10 and 12 years) and were boasting about which of them would 'shag them first', she put safety rules into operation but she was uncomfortable in discussing the behaviour, especially their use of crude language.

She had a very good record of settling difficult foster children so felt somewhat of a failure in the current situation. The first meeting did not make any progress so an agenda was drawn up for the next meeting with the aim of reducing Charlotte's anxiety as much as possible. Agenda items included:

- What support would be most helpful to Charlotte?

- What is her biggest worry?

- What 'unbreakable' rules work well in this foster family? And how can they be extended to the sexually concerning behaviour?

- How did her two (now grown-up) sons learn about sexual safety? And can this be applied to Adam and Jack?

- How much of the children's behaviour can she be responsible for? And how much responsibility should the children be encouraged to take?

Once sexually concerning behaviour is discovered, the daily routines of families change dramatically to address the need for increased safety. Examples of these changes include alternative sleeping arrangements, staggered bedtimes, the use of baby monitors and extended family being called upon to assist with supervision. When supplementary detail about the changes is also sought, for example, 'What does this say about your capacity to protect?' a narrative about the caring, responsible capabilities of the parents is developed and honoured. This in turn increases families' engagement from a 'just going along with it' position to a 'co-authoring the process' position. A further benefit is that families come to recognise that the behaviour can be spoken of in a way that reduces the feelings of shame for both the young person and the family: 'How it was separated helped. I'd tried everything. The Junction worker helped him find a name for it. That gave him an incentive. It would have been quicker to get through it if we'd had that earlier (parent quoted in *Safe Care Pack for Parents and Carers*, p.5).

In addition, once the parents have become accustomed to talking about the behaviour they are often able to initiate conversations about what has happened with their son/daughter. This in turn is a significant contribution to increased safety within the home.

Inevitably, this type of conversation can also result in the family demonstrating a lack of awareness about necessary changes or recognition that there is a need to make changes but a lack of capacity and/or confidence to implement them. This would increase concern and require consideration of alternative measures to increase levels of safety.

✎   **PRACTICE ACTIVITY**

Jerome's mother's mental health problems have necessitated her being admitted to hospital on several occasions, resulting in Jerome being looked after by the local authority four times. Mum has also had a series of partners, some of whom she met in hospital and who were dangerous and unstable, others whom she has allowed to take over her parental responsibilities. Her emotional instability has skewed her relationship with Jerome, which she describes as more like mates than mother and son. Jerome takes on responsibility for his mother's wellbeing (for example, he checks that she has taken her medication) whilst, at the same time, resenting that his needs are not always met. She has not established any safety measures to protect other children from Jerome, or him from allegations. Jerome is in the difficult position of having both too much and too little responsibility. When she is well, mum complains that he can be dominating but she abrogates responsibility when unwell. Jerome resents being disciplined by a succession of other parent figures, as he also resents school's efforts to implement safety measures, which he views as unreasonably restrictive.

- Look back at your list of concerns in this case. Does the information about Jerome's mother cause you to amend this list?

- What do you think needs to happen to keep both Jerome and other children safe?

Identifying what works in assisting the child/young person to avoid the sexually concerning behaviour

> When someone commits a crime and enters the justice system, two questions beg to be asked, 'How did you get into this mess?' and 'How can you get out of it?'...strengths based practitioners have begun to focus solely on the second question. (Clark 2013, p.133)

In adopting this position, Clark argues that you have to move the offender's view to centre stage: 'Why do we construct solutions solely from our point of view, when we are not the ones being asked to change?' (2013, p.134). One of the most useful things that the young person and family can bring to the conversation is their knowledge of what is already happening that is contributing towards increased safety. There is no set programme of work; the focus is on the person as an individual, utilising unique ways of working which are specific to them. The conversations concentrate on present and future functioning, rather than past failures.

Within the assessment there is a specific focus on gathering evidence about the skills, abilities and strengths and values evident in the young person and family's life. This is within the family home as well as the external context such as school, employment, clubs, etc. This is significant, particularly when their behaviour has led to them being pathologised and stigmatised. Such labelling can obscure any positive characteristics or narratives present in the life of the young person (Hackett 2004).

When there is a preoccupation with risk, the work can be consumed with finding problems. This can be a disempowering process for the family and can very quickly result in the family withdrawing from the process. This is disempowering for the worker too who is faced with a sharp increase in concerns. One way of counteracting this is to search for strengths and resources as identified by individual family members as well as those attributed by the professionals. Being interested and locating a family's unique strengths and abilities is a fundamental part of the approach and can quickly shift the dynamics of the work considerably. Families express surprise at our interest in these areas and at times need to be given some time to be able to practise thinking about how they have achieved success in other areas of their life. This process also puts into context the idea that the problems don't encroach into their whole life and this provides optimism and hope for the future. Useful questions include:

- Can you tell me something about your daughter that makes you proud as parents?

- How have you managed to carry on despite the recent upset and difficulties?

- What does this say about you as a family?

- What does it say about your strengths?

- What strengths would you identify as standing out in your family?

- Did you know that about yourself/your family?

- Can you tell me about other times where you have faced difficulties and specifically what you did which helped you to keep going?

- What ideas do you have about how these strengths and experiences can help you now?

Employing others in the quest to identify and authenticate people's strengths, resources and successes contributes significantly to the process. This includes everyone who has an interest in keeping children safe in each specific case – for example, other relatives with children, teachers, football coaches, etc. Identifying the strengths of individuals and families provides context to the current difficulties that they are experiencing, increases the likelihood that contact with professionals is a less threatening experience and makes 'forgotten' skills visible, which can then contribute towards increased levels of safety when transferred into future safety plans.

PRACTICE ACTIVITY

- Choose a child or young person who does not seem to have many redeeming qualities and then consult all the people in his or her life, asking them what positive qualities they have noticed about that person.

- Do any of these qualities hold potential for the development of safety?

Equally, assessments may be made which indicate insufficient levels of safety if the young person and family are unable to identify skills, strengths and abilities which can be drawn upon to increase safety in the future. It is important to remember that strengths do not in themselves equate with safety. But as skills and strengths are usually transferable within a range of situations, they are the building blocks from which safety is developed.

To agree a strategy for maintaining a problem-free future and to develop safety

All the people with concerns are encouraged to be active participants in the safety planning process, especially the child or young person whose behaviour gave rise to those concerns. This process includes:

- *A clear statement of the statutory agency's goals for the case in terms of what constitutes enough safety for the case to be closed.* This needs to be phrased in terms of what will be happening differently, not the absence of something. For example, Martin is a solitary 17-year-old who has a history of sexual touching since he was 12, hanging around shopping centres with older men and, more recently, using a camera phone in the girls' toilet of his care home. He has returned to another care home after a short youth custody sentence. Below are his and the professionals' goals.

Child/young person's goals: Martin wants to be trusted by staff. He has had a lot of moves in the care system and would like to settle down and make friends. He does not want to do anything that would mean he went back to prison.

Carers' goals: Martin's carers want him to be safe, more confident and make friends.

Professionals' goals: His social worker wants Martin to be taking responsibility for his behaviour and show that he is safe around other young people. He would also like him to have age-appropriate relationships.

- *Incorporating the family's strengths and resources as much as possible.* For example, six-year-old Kyle had become sexualised at a very early age following extensive sexual abuse by his parents and other adults. Now in foster care, he is exposing himself at school and touching other children on their private parts. His foster carer had identified that Kyle felt safest when his environment reminded him of the sea so she allowed him to sleep on the floor (his seabed) with blue covers and pictures of fish on three walls. On the fourth wall she began a 'good memories' wall where she displayed photographs of Kyle engaged in recent happy activities. This had reduced his nightmares and flashbacks significantly. Her creativity was utilised in tackling his sexualised behaviour at school; for example, she awarded him a fish sticker on a chart for every day he got through school without any sexual touching.

- *Encouraging things the family already does to create a safe environment, and drawing upon identified exceptions.* Charlotte instituted safe care rules to protect the girls: Adam and Jack were not allowed upstairs except when changing their school clothes and going to bed. They were to use the downstairs bathroom. She had also fitted a baby alarm but was tired of sleeping with 'one ear open' as the children's bedrooms were very close to each other so she was simply asked what would help most in this situation. She said she would like CCTV so her request for children's social care to fit this was supported. It was not intrusive as the children preferred it to the baby alarm.

- *Including the family's own safety ideas as much as possible.* Martin talked about having a switch in his head that allowed him to detach himself from what he is doing but how it had become a burden to him. Asking him about the times he had controlled the switch enabled him to identify several exceptions. These were the times he had remembered to take his insulin injections without reminder from staff and the times he had resisted self-harming, and the main way he had done this was taking a calming walk. Taking a calming walk became the first building block of Martin's responsibility-taking, which then quickly developed.

- *Drawing on the family's general goals if it is likely that they will increase the child's safety.* Adam's goal was that we (the professionals) would all stop making a fuss and go away. This is a helpful goal in that it enabled each professional to say what Adam needed to do before they would go away.

- *Always using those people who are willing (and able) to take action, especially trusted relatives and involved professionals.* These are not always the people professionals would identify. We often ask a child to make a *helping hand* by drawing round their hand and writing the names of people who they find most helpful and supportive on each digit. Who is left out is as informative as who is included. Some children have few trusted relatives and choose a pet or toy as a helper. For example, Kyle chose his goldfish as one helper.

- *Incorporating compliments where family members are already moving towards their own goals or goals of the agency.* Compliments need to be properly evidenced so that they can be owned by the family. Mostly we compliment by 'noticing' in our written feedback but occasionally add a further compliment. For example, Judith wrote in a covering letter: 'I could hardly believe what I had written when I read these notes. It is such an enormous amount of progress in a very short time. I hope you are both very pleased with yourselves.'

(adapted from Turnell and Edwards 1999, p.131)

Establishing the motivation and ability of participants to work towards safety

No matter how robust the agreed goals or plans may be, unless the young person and family are willing and able to work towards the agreed outcome then the likelihood is that this will not be achieved. This in turn will influence what assessment is made regarding levels of safety. Although the Signs of Safety model encourages young people to confront themselves, it is sensible to check out levels of motivation to change at an early stage. A useful way to begin this process is the use of scaling questions. Scaling questions offer versatility as they can be applied to any context, for example:

- If 1 is you can't be bothered to do anything about it (the harmful sexual behaviour) and 10 is you will do whatever it takes, where are you currently on this scale?

- What would need to happen for you to build upon this and move 1 point (or further) up the scale?

- You mentioned in your last session some ideas about keeping yourself safe from further allegations. On a scale of 1–10, how confident are you in your ability to do this?

- How confident are you in your child adhering to the agreed safety plan?

These scales contribute towards the assessment as well as promote dialogue about the young person's motivation to change and their ability to do this.

Recording the safety plan

Having followed the processes outlined in this chapter, the safety plan is then recorded and copies are given to all the interested parties. The safety plan is not a static document; it is updated regularly to detail evidence of progress or, where there has been no progress, to re-evaluate the safety plan. There is no one correct way of documenting the safety plan; it can take the form of a one-page chart or can be a more discursive document. You can devise your own scheme to fit your specific agency requirement and which suits the needs of the family best.

CASE EXAMPLE

This is the revised safety plan for looked-after Connor (16 years) when it became clear that he was making no progress in building safety at all.

Concerns ————————▶	Progress	Safety
1. Connor was sexually abused by his father and a female relative. He tells strangers about this, which makes him vulnerable to further abuse.		
2. Connor touched his brothers and sisters on their private parts.		3. Connor only has supervised contact with his brothers and sisters now.
4. Connor has learning difficulties that make it hard for him to understand how to keep safe.		
5. Connor breaks rules all the time. He enjoys doing this.	6. He has agreed to keep all rules. This is as yet untested.	
7. He has urges to touch kids aged 5 to 12 on their private parts.		
8. He has been alone with other young kids, even though he knows this is not allowed. His mum has taken him to his nan's where there are young kids.		9. Staff are now escorting him everywhere and he is only allowed to see his mum when supervised.

10. He understands what consent is but still intrudes on young people's personal space.		
11. He is disrespectful to his carers.		
12. He is not able to travel on public transport safely.		13. Staff are taking him to and from college and supervising him at break times.

Child/young person's goals	Carers' goals	Professionals' goals
Connor wants more freedom to go out with his friends on his own.	Staff want Connor to be safe enough around children so that he can have more freedom.	The social worker wants Connor to be safe enough around young children so that he can have more freedom.

Connor understands that what he did was wrong and knows how to control his urges but he doesn't bother to do this. He is disrespectful to staff and breaks rules designed to keep him from further allegations all the time. There are no signs of safety other than those imposed in terms of strict supervision, which must continue.

Signed	Signed	Signed

CASE EXAMPLE

After demonstrating increased safety in their home, Kieron and Lewis were allowed more freedom so contingency plans were added to the original safety plan to cover possible new risks.

Contingency safety plan
Safety plan for swimming
Sometimes Lewis doesn't feel safe when he and Kieron go to get changed for swimming. Mostly these situations don't arise but for the odd occasion, the family have decided:

- When changing for swimming, Kieron and Lewis will choose cubicles at opposite ends of the changing room.

- They will keep the curtains to the cubicles drawn.

- They will stay out of each other's cubicle.

The penalty for breaking the safety rules whilst in swimming changing rooms is that person will have to wash and dry everyone's swimming trunks.

Kieron and Lewis might as well start practising these safe care plans straight away – even when dad and mum are around.

Safety plan for the field at the back of the house and on the street
Only one boy is allowed in the field at a time after school (unless mum or dad is there).

- Kieron will have first go when he comes back from school so that he can kick a ball about to help keep him in a steady mood.

- Lewis will play out on the street. If his friends aren't there, he will come in and do homework or listen to music in his bedroom. He can go in the field after Kieron has left it.

- When anyone moves from field to bedroom, or street to bedroom, or upstairs to downstairs, they will check with mum and dad first so that mum and dad know where everyone is.

Safety plan for the donkey and bike sheds

The donkey shed and the bike shed will be padlocked.

- Dad will buy padlocks and be in charge of the keys.

- Kieron will unlock the donkey shed and put hay out for the donkey when he lets the dogs out each evening.

- Dad will lock the sheds.

 PRACTICE ACTIVITY

Complete the chart below for 12-year-old Hannah who is currently with foster parents, listing a constructive safe behaviour for each concern on the right hand side of the page. Avoid using the words 'don't' and 'not'.

Concerns	Safety
1. Hannah makes sexual overtures to children and young people	
2. She is physically aggressive to children and young people	
3. She steals from shops	
4. She swears at teachers	
5. When upset, she trashes her bedroom	

Summary

Where there is a preoccupation with risk, practice can become fixated on locating potential risk. A Signs of Safety model maintains a focus on the concerns whilst being structured around current and future safety. An assessment underpinned by solution-focused and narrative principles has a focus on the level of intervention required to assist the young person in maintaining a future that is free of sexually concerning and/or harmful behaviour. Establishing achievable and measurable goals is essential to the assessment process and increases the likelihood of positive outcomes. Goal setting should be undertaken with all concerned professionals, the young person and the family to provide clarity and expectations for all involved.

Gathering quality information about the alleged sexually concerning behaviour and the strengths, skills and resources of the family and exceptions to the harmful sexual behaviour provides depth and context to the situation that is being assessed. Clarifying the understanding and position of each individual with regard to the harmful sexual behaviour and involving the young person, family and professionals are important parts of the safety planning process.

CHAPTER 4

Conversations with Young People about their Behaviour

This chapter describes strengths-based techniques which encourage constructive conversations about issues of consent, power, coercion, responsibility-taking and respectfulness to increase engagement with young people and their families with the aim of encouraging active participation in change and a move towards future safety. Alternative and different responses and positions that can be held when working with a young person, including denial of the behaviour, are also described. In addition, other media for use with young people who are difficult to engage are described.

Talking about the behaviour

Young people usually find it difficult to talk about their sexually concerning behaviour for a number of reasons; they may be fearful of legal and social consequences and/or feel ashamed and embarrassed. Even in the context of child protection and future safety it is both important and helpful to engage at any level of conversation that the young person is willing to have at that time. We have found that once some communication is established these conversations will often expand into others and it is at this point that we recognise the importance of influencing what we talk about.

Historically, within the field of criminal justice the emphasis has been on ascertaining the rationale for a person's behaviour. This interest in causality has often resulted in conversations about safety being lost. In contrast a strengths-based approach shows an interest in how a young person has demonstrated safer behaviour in the past and how they are going to do more of this in future. The Signs of Safety approach provides a framework where the safety of the victim and/or alleged victim and others is consistently reviewed and remains as a focus of the work, but this is achieved within a context where the young person is viewed as a young person who has displayed harmful sexual behaviour and not regarded as a 'mini' sex offender. That is, we view the young person as a person *with* a problem not a person who *is* a problem. This has the benefit of placing them at the centre of the intervention but without viewing them as defined entirely by their harmful sexual behaviour.

This strengths-based practice concentrates on increasing levels of safety and views the young person as the expert in their life; each person knows best how to create and take responsibility for future safety – as Clark says, 'why do we construct solutions solely from our point of view, when we are not the ones being asked to change?' (2013, p.134). The role of the worker is to aid the young person in talking about the harmful sexual behaviour and work together to identify strengths, abilities and resources that increase their capacity to manage the behaviour alongside working towards an alternative preferred future of increased safety. This shifts the dynamics of the working relationship from one which is authoritarian, with the worker's position and knowledge being privileged and given substance, into one that respects the young people's accounts and knowledge whilst promoting increased responsibility for their behaviour and future safety. Needless to say, the approach ensures that the harmful behaviour is not minimised. This should not be seen as a 'soft option'. That would result in professional dangerousness. At no point is the harmful behaviour either minimised or condoned; there is an expectation that the young person will take responsibility for their behaviour and their own and others' future safety.

Thus a strengths-based perspective ditches the common adversarial style of offender management for a relationship where cooperation and respect are nurtured. This is not simply a humane response; it is one that has been demonstrated to be most effective. A confrontational style of working has been found to limit effectiveness (Hubble, Duncan and Miller 1999; Miller and Rollnick 2002). Miller, Benefield and Tonnigan (1993) discovered that a directive–confrontational style of working resulted in resistance increasing twofold. The importance of maintaining a flexible and creative approach becomes imperative when a child or young person is embarrassed, ashamed or frightened about discussing the behaviour. As practitioners we expect this to happen and work alongside the child to create ways of moving forward. At the same time we are transparent about our hopes for the work and what needs to be different for us to be confident that there is sufficient safety for the case to be closed. Equally there are some things that we don't do, such as:

- interpret or check what they are saying against a favourite theory

- ask why – if children knew why they were doing something, they either wouldn't do it or would be embarrassed to admit they did

- use questionnaires or worksheets – these not only constrict the limits of the conversation, but also children tell us that they don't like doing them.

(Milner and Bateman 2011, p.37)

Responses to the behaviour

When harmful sexual behaviour comes to the attention of family and any legal processes commence, we experience a range of responses from young people with regards to their ability to communicate about their behaviour. Whilst exception finding is central to our approach, it is rare that we can talk about this at initial contact as it would involve the young person accepting what they had done. First we need to be able to talk about the concerns and the young person and family's responses to these before we can begin to make assessments of future safety.

I DIDN'T DO IT!

Harmful sexual behaviour with a child under the age of 13 is an absolute offence which carries serious consequences in the short term – a possible custodial sentence, and in the longer term, the status as a Schedule One Offender. Not surprisingly, denial is a common response although historically denial has been, and still is, considered to be an indicator of risk despite denial and minimisation being very common human behaviours.

✎ **PRACTICE ACTIVITY**

• Think back to a time when taking full responsibility for an action would have had legal or financial consequences, such as a bump in your car, a lost piece of jewellery, accidental damage to a carpet.

• Were you able to accept responsibility for the action or did you deny or minimise events?

• What were the drivers for your responses?

A problem-solving approach works hard to find who is responsible, where the problem comes from and how it is maintained. Accountability is achieved when the offender can admit their guilt. However, research suggests that although acknowledgement of responsibility of abuse is preferable, it is neither a sufficient nor necessary condition of safety (Turnell and Edwards 1999, p.40). Judith has worked with a number of adults whose behaviour was sexually harmful and were able to admit their guilt and express remorse, often accompanied by copious tears. She found that, as with people who are abusive towards their partners, this in itself did not assure future safety. Instead, the strengths-based perspective argues that an admission of guilt does not demand accountability for future safety; it can only be demonstrated by active change in the young person's behaviour. Questions that bypass denial include:

• What is more important to you, to be believed that you didn't do it, or to get out of this mess you are in?

• You say you are safe around children, so what hard evidence of your safe behaviour is there that will convince the judge?

When working with other professionals who are concerned about a young person's denial of the behaviour it is helpful to highlight the possible reasons why the young person may have taken this position. Equally, families can deny that the behaviour has happened or acknowledge that something did happen but struggle to believe that their child was involved.

✏ PRACTICE ACTIVITY

Nine-year-old Lucy is found by her parents crying on the stairs. She said a man had got into her bed and 'put his willy into' her, which hurt. He then left out of the bedroom window. Police investigation finds semen on her underwear; the DNA matches that of her 13-year-old brother Paul. By the time we are asked to become involved, the boy had been sent by children's social care to live in a foster home 53 miles away. He is not allowed to have any contact with young people. This means he is not allowed out, except in his foster carer's company. He cannot attend school. There are no other young people in the foster home. He is not allowed unsupervised contact with his family, or to talk to them on the phone. Meanwhile, his sister is repeatedly saying that it was a stranger who perpetrated the attack. Her family believes her, but children's social care do not. The case does not go to court because there is a problem with the DNA evidence (Bateman and White 2008).

- In what way would breaking down the denial help you move the work forward?

- Would it make any difference if the boy admitted guilt but his sister and mother maintained their denial?

- List the possible reasons why each family member may be taking the position they do.

In the context of denial, Jenkins (1990) makes the point that whilst you can't make someone take responsibility, you can invite them to do so. The tradition of invitation reminds a worker to provide opportunities for the young person to make choices, the challenge being to help young people confront themselves. Furthermore, it is helpful to view this process as gradual and fluid and one that changes and develops over time in contrast to it being fixed. Where family members support the denial, Jenkins recommends working with parents and carers initially, suggesting that some slight movement is required by the family or the young person may struggle to take responsibility for their future behaviour. Maintaining neutrality, considering the accounts of both the young person who has displayed the behaviour and the young person who has been harmed, is a helpful position to take. This avoids conflicting conversations about who is to blame, which can be a barrier to constructive work. We concentrate on assessing the knowledge, motivation and capabilities of the young person to display safer sexual behaviours, gathering evidence of how and when they have demonstrated more appropriate behaviour.

Despite the denial there is still a need to engage the young person in an assessment of their understanding of consent, power, respect, victim empathy and responsibility to keep safe from further allegations. But often this doesn't happen, and workers get stuck in attempting to break down denial as the report *Examining Multi-agency Responses to Children and Young People who Sexually Offend* (Criminal Justice Joint Inspection 2013) discovered. It found that little intervention was undertaken when the harmful sexual behaviour was denied, resulting in a lack of assessments being made. This, in turn, could put others at risk of continuing harm and neglect the needs of the young person. As well as inviting responsibility-taking (Jenkins 1990, 2005a), the Resolutions Approach, developed by Essex (Turnell and Essex 2006) bypasses the denial impasse in work with adults, although we find it works equally well with young people. Essex devised a strategy whereby 'similar but different' stories are created that mirror the behaviour detailed in the allegations. The similar but different process:

- creates a context where parents can talk about abuse without getting into denial stories and disputation (can't be used against them in court as it's not the real family)

- allows the non-abusing parent to consider other possibilities and strengthen the protective role

- creates a context where trust, responsibility, impact on children, etc. can be discussed in detail
- allows the exploration of difficult relational dynamics
- looks at all people's perspectives, including the wider family's.

It enables an exploration of the issues relating to this type of behaviour, within a neutral context which avoids blame and conflict. An assessment is made of a young person's understanding in relation to these issues through an activity that respects their position of denial whilst challenging their understanding of what constitutes safe, respectful behaviour. During a similar but different scenario, questions can be asked such as:

- How may this girl be feeling whilst the behaviour is happening?
- How may this girl be feeling afterwards?
- How may this boy be feeling whilst the behaviour is happening?
- How may this boy be feeling afterwards?
- What first steps could these parents take to begin to increase safety in the home?
- How should they respond to the needs of their daughter?
- What impact may the behaviour have on this boy's relationship with his family?
- How can trust be rebuilt? How long will this take?
- What needs to happen so this girl can start to feel safe?

Creating these scenarios and initiating conversations that acknowledge impact and safety allows qualities and abilities to emerge that may have been previously hidden. One parent said that seeing it from the outside looking in made it easier to talk about the issues with each other (Gumbleton 1997, p.57). And, 'many difficult conversations became possible on the basis that this is what the Court or Child Protection Case Conference would expect us to consider, in order to fulfil the carers' responsibility for children's future safety' (Essex and Gumbleton 1999, p.140).

PRACTICE ACTIVITY

Using 'similar but different' scenarios with families is complex and requires a great deal of preparation both on the part of the worker and with the family. Before embarking on hypothetical work with a family:

- Read Chapter 8 of *Working with 'Denied' Child Abuse. The Resolutions Approach* (Turnell and Essex 2006).

- Using the scenario of the nine-year-old girl outlined earlier in this chapter, plan how you would prepare this family for a 'similar but different' role play.

'That's not fair!'

When young people display harmful sexual behaviour they are expected to take responsibility for such behaviour, be accountable to those towards whom their behaviour has been displayed and – eventually – acknowledge and demonstrate an understanding of the harm that their behaviour has caused. These expectations can often be within a context where their own experiences of harm and victimisation have been unchallenged, unacknowledged and dismissed. This imbalance of justice can result in professionals juggling a moral and ethical conflict as well as young people being labelled resistant when they protest against systems which expect them to take responsibility when others have not had to take responsibility for what has been done to them. We would argue that we can't expect young people to show respect to others if we don't demonstrate respectfulness towards them.

CASE EXAMPLE

Twelve-year-old Noah has a history of impulsive, aggressive and criminal behaviour as well as sexually concerning behaviour. The former consists of things such as climbing on the roofs of teachers' cars, the latter mainly of making inappropriate comments to girl pupils although there was an (unproven) allegation of the rape of a young child. He is currently in foster care, his background being one of neglect, exposure to domestic violence, criminal and substance misuse activities, and repeated separations from his mother who makes little effort to contact him. Noah is completely unable to talk about his sexually concerning behaviour; he simply and briefly denies it. Neither does he talk about his thoroughly miserable earlier life.

What Noah can talk about is his sense of injustice at being excluded from school. He says it's not fair as the girls to whom he is accused of making inappropriate comments bullied him and nothing happened to them. Acknowledging this unfairness led to an interesting conversation about how he had prevented one girl from being bullied, which in turn led to a conversation about how he does respectfulness and what would be happening when his mother is being more respectful to him.

Note: When talking with children we adopt the narrative technique of using reflexive verbs or verbs ending in 'ing' as nouns – for example, 'How do you do self-calming?' (Freeman *et al.* 1997, p.114). This creates a relationship between the person and the behaviour that implies that children can learn about themselves from themselves.

'OK, I did it, but I don't want to talk about it'

There are times when we meet with a young person who admits that they did sexually harm another person but they just want it all to go away. They are not ready to talk about the behaviour so professionals need to respect this position if they hope to make progress in building safety. It is possible to do some preparatory work around 'talking' and how we plan for this, asking questions such as:

- What would help you to feel more ready or able to talk about the behaviour?

- Are there some things that you are happy to talk about now and other things that we can discuss later on?

- Can you tell me about times when 'talking' has been useful. What were the effects of that talking?

- Who have you found to be the best person to talk to?

- Is there someone who you have already discussed the behaviour with that I can talk with and then for us to meet after that?

- How about we plan today what we are going to discuss and then start the talking bit when we next meet?

When we have discussed with young people at the end of the work what their initial reservations were for not wanting to participate in the work, they often recall their anxieties that we were going to be very shaming and critical of them because this is what they have experienced previously. We also find that these children reject praise as they habitually do criticism. Others are rendered silent by shame and embarrassment, or a lack of language to talk about what they have done.

Shame and embarrassment

 PRACTICE ACTIVITY

Think about a time when you did something that you were aware was wrong and when this action or behaviour was discovered you denied your involvement. Hold that memory in your mind whilst you continue to read the following section.

Talking about harmful sexual behaviour can be a difficult process, particularly when a young person is embarrassed and/or ashamed about what they have done. When it is shame that has made it difficult,

Jenkins (2005b) suggests it is most constructive to acknowledge the shame and use it to move forwards by asking questions such as:

- What does it say about you that you are ashamed of having done this?
- What would it say about you if you were not ashamed?

Where embarrassment is the main hindrance to talking about the concerns, the use of games can be helpful, as long as they are suitably adapted.

CASE EXAMPLE

Twelve-year-old James had been displaying sexually concerning behaviour towards his seven-year-old brother. During the initial sessions James explained that he felt embarrassed talking about sex and sexual behaviour. When Jackie asked him, 'What needs to be different for us to do the work?' James suggested that games might help. Jackie knew of a game designed by another young person and so she asked James if he would help her to update it for an older young person by reviewing the questions used in the game. James agreed to this and he acted as a 'consultant'. This involved him in reading all the questions which related to sex, puberty and appropriate behaviours, then giving his opinion on their suitability for a 12-year-old. This enabled Jackie to assess James's knowledge and challenge him where required without embarrassing him in the process. There was a positive outcome in that James not only later demonstrated safety but also contributed to making a new resource which could then be used in his school environment in 'circle time' to reinforce the messages he had learned about appropriate sexual behaviours in the work.

CASE EXAMPLE

Ryan (seven years old) was referred to The Junction for using sexual references and touching children at school. Ryan expressed embarrassment when talking about private parts of the body; however, he enjoyed playing games with the worker who designed a card game called 'Body Part Snap' and used it with Ryan to encourage his participation and learning regarding body parts and which ones are private.

It is not only children who are embarrassed when talking about sexual behaviour; adults often find it embarrassing to use vernacular terms for body parts and acts. They distance themselves from the embarrassment by using strictly biological terms or euphemisms, commonly talking about 'inappropriate' behaviour. However, in detailing the concerns and in checking the accuracy of these, workers need to be able to check with young people what words their peer groups commonly use for words such as penis, vagina, erection, etc. We find that it helps to rehearse a possible vocabulary with colleagues before meeting with the young person.

 PRACTICE ACTIVITY

Think back to the earlier question about locating a time when you didn't admit to doing something you knew to be wrong. Now imagine that the person who asked about your involvement could read your mind and was actually aware that you did do what you were denying.

- How would you feel?
- What would you be concerned about?
- What would you be scared of?

✎ **PRACTICE ACTIVITY**

You are talking to nine-year-old Billy in your workplace when his school bag tips over, spilling some books onto the floor. As you help him pick them up, a loose leaf drops out of a school exercise book. It is covered with a well-executed, neatly coloured drawing of two ninja turtles in full battle dress. To your horror, it is evident that one ninja is having anal intercourse with the other whilst brandishing a sword.

- How would you respond to this discovery?
- Having had time to think about it, what words and phrases would you use in a later conversation with Billy about the drawing?

What's the problem?

Unfortunately, some young people live in circumstances where abusive behaviour is such a part of their daily routine that their ability to differentiate between appropriate and abusive behaviours is impaired. Distinguishing the difference between harmful sexual behaviour and age-appropriate sexual behaviour and then shifting a young person's perspective and understanding can be a difficult and challenging task.

CASE EXAMPLE

Niall touches girls and boys, exposes his private parts, goes into the girls' toilet and messes about in lessons in his primary school class. He understands now that this is wrong and is troubled by his impulse to keep doing it. He says that the *touching problem* happens mostly at school; he doesn't do it as much in his foster home.

He knows which are boys' private parts, and which are girls' private parts. He thinks he understands the difference between good and bad secrets but this also troubles him. When his foster carer explained the difference between good and bad secrets by giving the example of a family surprise party as a good secret, Niall then told her that his birth family had 'naughty parties'. He didn't want to tell her about these parties because he didn't want to upset her.

Families and professionals often tell us that they are unsure how serious the concerning behaviour actually is; is it just kids mucking about? The underlying factors which determine whether a young person's sexual behaviour is appropriate or not relate to the presence of consent, coercion and power. Consent refers to:

- the person has an understanding of the sexual behaviour that is being proposed.
- awareness of the societal ethics related to the behaviour
- knowledge of the potential consequences
- shared respect for agreements or disagreements related to the behaviour
- being mentally competent
- voluntary participation in the behaviour.

(adapted from Ryan and Lane, 1997, pp.4–5)

Children under 13 cannot legally consent to sexual activity and the offences under sections 5, 6, 7 and 8 do not require proof of consent (Sexual Offences Act 2003).

Under the terms of the Mental Capacity Act 2005, incapacity is regarded as being unable to make a particular decision if a person is unable to:

- understand the information relevant to the decision
- retain that information in their mind
- use or weigh up that information as part of the decision-making process
- communicate that decision by whatever means they have available.

(Brindle et al. 2013)

In simple terms, an individual cannot consent without knowing fully what they are being asked to do. Equally, they must be able to understand that they can decline from participating or change their mind and stop. Thus consent differs from compliance and cooperation. Compliance is when a child allows something to happen despite their own beliefs and desires, and cooperation is participation in the behaviour regardless of their own beliefs or desires. These are important distinctions as some young people will argue that the victim participated fully or even instigated the activity. A child may engage fully in sexual behaviour because they have been sexualised by earlier abuse or they may have mixed feelings of sexual arousal and disgust.

Equality of power within relationships is also a factor to take account of. There can be obvious signs of differences in power such as size, age, intellect and positions of power, and more subtle signs such as an individual's strength or popularity. With power often comes coercion, 'the pressures that deny the victim free choice including power and size differences, bribery, threats, and overt violence' (Ryan and Lane 1997, pp.5). This can range from threats to tell if the secret isn't kept to the offer of sweets as a bribe. A helpful way to distinguish between harmful sexual behaviour and age-appropriate sexual behaviour is to consider the following questions:

- Has the sexual behaviour put another person at risk of physical danger or impacted on their emotional, intellectual or mental health?
- Is the behaviour against the law?
- Have all parties been able to provide true consent?
- Has any form of power and coercion been present in the interaction and/or relationship?
- Has the sexual behaviour resulted in the young person feeling distressed, embarrassed or confused?

Talking about consent, coercion and power can be straightforward – for example, 'What do you mean when you say it was just a bit of fooling around?' or it can be complex where there appears to be cooperation and compliance. Talking about consent can be made easier when the relevant issues are explored in a game. Workers at Barnardo's The Junction adapted a Snakes and Ladders board game for this purpose.

The game involves first of all reading the pertinent sections from *Sex and the Law in England and Wales* (leaflet available from the Sheffield Centre for HIV). The adapted version of Snakes and Ladders is used to check how well the young person understands consent and the law. The standard board is used, but if either the young person or the worker lands on a snake or a ladder then the young person has to read one of the specially prepared cards (see Figure 4.1) and say whether consent has truly been given, or not. If the young person answers correctly, it means:

- the young person can go up the ladder
- the young person does not have to go down the snake
- the worker cannot go up the ladder
- the worker has to go down the snake.

The hope is that the young person wins the game by demonstrating an understanding of the concept of consent – and has fun being competitive in the process.

The conversation can be expanded by asking other questions in each scenario, such as:

- What could happen next?
- Who has power here?
- What is being consented to?
- Are enough details known?
- What would happen if they said *no*?
- What do the people in this scenario feel?
- What could they do?

This begins to demonstrate the young person's level of understanding of the concept of consent by their ability to identify situations where consent had not been given by a child because of their age or as a result of bribery, trickery, force and coercion and/or other influences and factors such as drugs and alcohol or learning disability. Such scenarios also bring into conversations the presence of power in relationships and how people can use power to influence their participation in situations to which they have not consented. Junction worker Carol Larne, says:

Every time I've used this activity I've 'seen the light go on', even with children as young as eight or nine, in which case the scenarios need re-phrasing; for example, use the words 'touching' instead of 'penetrating', 'licking', etc. and 'privates' instead of 'penis', 'vagina' (Personal communication 2013).

A 17-year-old girl, Jo, makes Adam (aged 10) touch his penis while she watches.	Paul, Kyle and Kylie are 12. They often visit Martin's house. He is 32. He lets them watch pornography and drink beer.	Samantha is 14. She took 2 ecstasy pills at a party and had sex with 3 guys who were all aged 16.
Amanda is 14. She masturbates whilst her cousins (aged 7 and 8) are playing in the same room.	Aiden is 10. He agrees to have anal sex with Sam, aged 16.	Sally is 11. She has learning difficulties. She has touched her friend Daniel's penis because he said she had to or he would break her PlayStation.

Figure 4.1 Consent activity cards

We have also used established board games such as Man's World as a way of assessing a young man's knowledge, value base and position on a variety of issues such as sexual health knowledge, relationships, sex and sexuality, and friendships. The game has three types of cards, *What if?*, *Chance* and *True/False* questions. On the back of each question is a section of a man's body which, if answered correctly, is kept by the young person to build into an outline of a 'complete man'. There are additional questions on the board itself, such as 'What would you most like to change about your personality?' or 'Tell the group something that you've done that you're proud of.'

The *What if?* questions are constructed to encompass typical dilemmas which young people meet in their sexual and social relationships – for example, 'What would you do if your mates offered you a ride in a stolen car?' 'What would you do if your mum came in while you were wanking?' 'What would you do if your mates didn't like the person you're going out with?' 'What if your mate is being abused by his dad?'

The *True/False* questions are factual statements – for example, 'A 14-year-old boy is too young to be charged with raping someone.' These provide a platform to deepen the discussion – for example, 'Surfing the net for porn is a natural thing for blokes to do.' Accessibility to pornography through the internet is a huge issue for young people today. It is becoming increasingly recognised that viewing pornography at an early age is detrimental to a child's development (Horvath *et al.* 2013). Studies conducted with young people have reported that regular viewing of pornography has led to early sexual experiences, with young people trying out the sexual acts they have seen in pornography (Häggström-Nordin *et al.* 2009). Negative feelings including shame, distress, guilt and anger have also been reported (Flander, Cosic and Profaca 2009). Talking about sexually concerning behaviour needs thoughtfulness to avoid one-sided lectures about right and wrong but the *True/False* questions facilitate talk about keeping safe, the impact on young people of viewing pornography, and the law. They also challenge 'lad lore', the often inaccurate knowledge exchanged between young people.

The *Chance* questions are a mixture of true/false statements coupled with more open-ended questions, which again provide an opportunity to explore the subject area in greater depth – for example, 'What does safer sex mean?' Such a question can generate conversations about sexual health and sexually transmitted diseases, responsibility and consent.

Whilst this game is specifically designed to encourage young men to communicate and share their feelings and experiences and opinions as well as increase their sexual knowledge, some slight tweaking enables it to be played with young women too. Equally, it is a useful resource to play with colleagues to practise communicating about these issues, as well as feeling more comfortable with sexual language and development of sexual knowledge. Magazines are also a good source of discussion on sexual knowledge and relationship dilemmas; adolescent publications often contain information and advice that recognises the importance of consent and communication within relationships (Quillam 2005). With very young children we have used specially adapted Mr Men and Little Miss figures. These are also useful when working with young people with learning difficulties so will be discussed more fully in Chapter 6.

PRACTICE ACTIVITY

- List the resources available to you in your agency.
- List your specific skills in communicating with children.
- Using these resources and skills, design a 'game' that will be useful in your work context.

Summary

Many young people find it difficult to talk about their sexually concerning behaviour, so it is worthwhile engaging in any conversation they find comfortable before expanding into more safety-related conversations when engagement is more established. This can be achieved by using a Signs of Safety framework, which ensures that the safety of others remains central to the work but where the young person is not defined by their harmful sexual behaviour.

Denial is considered by many professionals to be an indicator of risk. However, research suggests that acknowledgement of guilt is neither an adequate nor required condition of safety. A strengths-based perspective argues that accountability for future safety can only be demonstrated by active change in a person's behaviour. To encourage a young person to show responsibility for their (mis-) behaviour it is helpful for the young person to experience being respected, particularly when they themselves have also been victims.

The factors determining whether a young person's sexual behaviour is appropriate or not depend on the presence of consent, coercion and abuses of power. An individual cannot provide consent to something unless they completely understand what they are being asked to do. Compliance refers to an individual allowing something to happen regardless of their beliefs or desires, and cooperation is engagement in an activity regardless of beliefs or desires.

CHAPTER 5

Working with Families

This chapter highlights the importance of working with all family members – immediate and extended, birth and foster parents – to increase safety. How parents' and carers' reactions to the sexually concerning behaviour influence their ability to safeguard is discussed, as well as the levels of support needed. The chapter also describes and illustrates how to begin safe care planning and construct safe care plans.

Involving parents and carers

Whilst it may be necessary to undertake some direct work with the young person whose behaviour is sexually concerning, it is essential that work is delivered in the context of the whole family. Both clinical and research literature (Friedrich 2007; Johnson 1989, 2004; Silvosky *et al.* 2007) has emphasised the involvement of parents/carers and other significant adults in the child's life. This includes working with teachers and other educational staff, especially where the behaviour has been displayed within school or other educational settings (classroom safety is more fully discussed in Chapter 7). A child's sexually concerning behaviour may be a reflection of their family and social environment and these are therefore prominent areas that need to be considered when assessing levels of safety, especially where moral, social and emotional boundaries are blurred or non-existent. Even where the home environment does not have a direct bearing on the behaviour, families need to be engaged in the safety planning process to increase the likelihood of sustained changes in the child's behaviour.

The family is a potential resource for both the young person and involved professionals, with the family providing information about the young person's needs and resources. Information about how the family members demonstrate, or fail to demonstrate, respect and responsibility towards each other, how privacy is managed within the home, beliefs and values regarding sex and sexuality as well as the family's coping strategies have a significant bearing on understanding the young person and their environment during the assessment/intervention process. First though, families need time to digest the news that the child they care for has sexually harmed, or has the potential to harm other children.

Reactions to the news

Harmful sexual behaviour on the part of a child or young person poses a powerful threat to a family's sexual safety and throws up questions about parenting ability. The impact of the behaviour can be evident across the various domains of their life, from how a parent feels about their child, their questioning of their ability to be a parent, their relationships with partners and other family members, and the routines and practicalities of everyday life. Research into foster carers' responses found that they feel a range of emotions, including feeling frightened, humiliated, shocked, betrayed, guilty, incompetent and hopeless (Milner 2008). Our experience in working with birth families found they almost all reacted to the news that their child had harmed another – often also their child – a devastating and isolating experience. One mother told us:

> Before the police came, I lived in fear of what might happen… I lived in fear of the problem being known by the community and what might happen. I used to sneak out of the house at night and spend my time upstairs. My child was getting bullied at school and I realized the problem had got out. He was off school for some time. ('Helen', cited in Milner 2006)

Parents, not surprisingly, hope to keep the problem a secret from neighbours but the question of who needs to know must be addressed to ensure the safety of all children, not just the ones involved in a particular incident. This can be discussed in terms of what measures need to be put in place to ensure not only the safety of children generally but also the safety of the offender from further allegations.

There is often a sense of disbelief and puzzlement: 'Where does it come from, this behaviour? I thought I'd brought them up well enough for them to know right from wrong. He must have known it was wrong' (parent cited in Barnardo's 2005, p.9). And the reaction is sometimes one of outright denial, which makes it difficult to involve parents in safe care planning. Whatever the different and difficult positions, responses and questions that parents and others adopt, professionals have to manage these sensitively whilst ensuring that sufficient levels of safety for all concerned remain central to the work.

✎ PRACTICE ACTIVITY

Looking back at the example of a nine-year-old girl found crying on the stairs (see Chapter 4), what words would you use to show these parents that you understand the position they have taken whilst still ensuring the safety of their daughter?

Parents and carers also begin to worry about what is 'normal'. Friends and family often rush to downplay the significance of the incident, ascribing it to 'normal experimentation'. This isn't helpful to a parent struggling to make sense of their child's behaviour: 'Knowing when a problem becomes a problem, that it's not just part of growing up. When the line gets crossed. That's the problem' (parent cited in Barnardo's 2005, p.7). In our experience it is important at the beginning of the work with families that their child's behaviour is put into context. Often, words such as 'abusive', 'harmful' or 'inappropriate' are used to explain the behaviour but families can often be left confused by the way their child's behaviour has been defined: 'Social Services said it was normal family behaviour but I knew it wasn't right' (parent cited in Barnardo's 2005, p.7). 'Normal' sexual behaviour can easily be explained by using a chart that lists a continuum of sexual behaviours as the basis for a discussion about their own child's behaviour.

Table 5.1 Sexual Behaviour Continuum

Behaviour	Expected Sexual Play	Innapropriate Sexual Behaviours	Abusive Sexual Behaviours
Coercion	Seldom	Seldom	Typical
Age Difference	Little	Little	Considerable
Mutual Involvement/ Initiation	Typical	Sometimes	Seldom
Type of Behaviour	Exploratory. Does not involve adult-like behaviours	Varies, but may involve adult-like behaviours	Varies, but may involve adult-like behaviours
Associated Emotion	Usually no serious distress at the time	Possibly embarrassment, fear, guilt and shame. Not traumatic	Possibly embarrassment, fear, guilt, shame and traumatic
Duration	Intermittent	Varies	Varies

Adapted from Ryan and Blum (1994) by L. Webster for Barnardo's The Junction

Talking about the behaviour

There are several difficulties to be overcome in establishing constructive conversations about safety between parents and children; adults often find it more embarrassing to talk about sexual matters than children do. When they decide to talk to their children about the behaviour, they worry about how to begin, and having started talking to their child, they are soon at a loss when the child laughs it off or refuses to discuss it. Parents who designed and wrote their own guide (*Safe Care: A Guide for Parents of Children who Sexually Offend*), offer this advice:

> Start by listening to your child again. This sounds obvious but many parents find they have so many confusing feelings and thoughts about the situation that they are either not listening at all, or lecturing. You do need to tell your child that what they

have done is wrong but that you still love them and will stick at helping them make sure that it doesn't happen again. If your child is denying it happened, let them know you understand that they may be too ashamed, embarrassed or afraid to admit what they have done. Let your child know that you still value them. Whatever they have done, this is only part of their behaviour and they will still be doing lots of things right. It is important to remember these. Tell them what things they do that make you proud of them and draw up a list. (Barnardo's 2005, pp.11–12)

The difficulties professionals face in talking with parents include embarrassment in talking about sexual matters, lack of vocabulary and – most of all – fear that they will be branded unfit and the child will be removed from their care. As discussed earlier in the book, 'externalising' – a technique where the young person is separated from the problem behaviour through a naming process – has been found to be both powerful and empowering to the family by providing them with a vocabulary to communicate about the harmful sexual behaviour (see, for example, Myers et al. 2003). Parents find it helpful when their parenting successes are acknowledged. As with the advice to parents on talking with their children (above), they are still doing lots of things right and it is important to remember these.

The issue of communication and, particularly, increasing both the quantity and quality of communication is a significant focus of our work with families. This is not just about the behaviour but how as a family they communicate with each other generally and in specific contexts – for example, how do they demonstrate respect to each other? Equally, we demonstrate this both subtly through how we communicate with them and more directly through the use of Strength cards[1] and games such as Respect and Responsibility Bingo[2] which can facilitate discussions on how as parents they model respectful behaviour towards each other.

---

1   www.innovativeresources.org
2   www.marcoproducts.com

PRACTICE ACTIVITY

Read Celia's story below:

> I am female, 40 and a single parent of a son who is 14.
>
> Approximately two years ago I found out my son had been involved in inappropriate behaviour with my niece who is quite a few years younger than him. My son has never denied what had happened.
>
> When I found out it was as if the bottom had dropped out of my world. I was worried that Social Services would take my son away, that he would be locked up, I would be branded an unfit mother and that the family would start taking sides. I was hurt because I thought that me and my son were close, could talk about anything and were honest with each other. I also felt very, very ashamed. To make things worse, I had been ill during the time this was taking place and it was my sister and her family that had supported me through it all.
>
> I worked at the time at a university and now for the NHS. I worry about my colleagues finding out because I fear being judged. At first I feared my son would never be able to follow his career path and become a teacher.
>
> I believed life would never be the same again. (Celia, cited in Milner 2006)

Plan how you would respond to Celia's distress. What words would you use?

Safe care planning

Whilst we take the position that the young person who has displayed harmful sexual behaviour is responsible for their own actions, we recognise that working with that young person to take responsibility for their own and others' safety can take time. In the short term, a home safety plan is required where family members take a leading role by clarifying family rules, developing boundaries and increasing supervision within the home. In assessing the potential of parents' and carers' capability and willingness to undertake this safety role, Chaffin *et al.* (2008) suggest the following factors should be considered:

- the capacity of the parent/carer to supervise and monitor
- the quality of the relationship between parent/carer and child
- the presence of any physical, emotional and sexually inappropriate behaviour within the home
- the presence of negative or positive role models and peers in the child's social environment
- the warmth and support provided to the child
- types of structure, limits, discipline, or consequences applied; the level of disciplinary consistency; and the child's response
- the development of factors related to resilience, or strengths and resources that can be developed
- access to opportunities for inappropriate behaviour
- extent and degree of violent and or sexual stimulation to the past and current environment
- exposure to, and protection from, potentially traumatic situations
- cultural factors of the community and home

(adapted from Chaffin *et al.* 2008, p.203)

The presence, or absence, of these factors influences the safety building process – for example, where there are good parent–child relationships, the parents are more likely to embrace safety planning. Where there are fewer protective factors, more work on engaging the parents is required and/or the involvement of other relatives, such as visiting aunts and uncles who can provide additional sets of eyes and ears. Where there are no protective factors, external safeguards will be necessary; and where an existing protective factor is removed – for example, the illness of a supportive parent – again, safety is compromised.

CASE EXAMPLE

Twelve-year-old Ashley is currently accommodated in a children's home following the discovery that he sexually assaulted a nine-year-old girl he had enticed into his home on the pretext that his little sister had asked her to come over to play. His mother has been re-housed in a different part of the city after neighbours threatened her and her daughter, culminating in a brick being thrown through her window. Ashley has been enrolled at a different secondary school but has refused to attend since he discovered that a boy in his year is related to a family near his old address. He sees his mother and sister for two hours at weekends. This visit is supervised by a worker from his children's home. This worker reports that the quality of these visits is not good as Ashley's mother is often inebriated.

Ashley refuses to talk about his sexual offending or engage in the assessment process in any way. His mother is requesting that Ashley be allowed to spend weekends with her, including sleepovers. Despite smelling strongly of alcohol, she insists that she hasn't 'touched a drop in weeks'.

Comment
Not surprisingly, Ashley's home visits continued to be supervised.

Where parents seem reluctant or resistant, scaled questions can be used to assess and develop confidence, willingness and capacity to change. For example, on a scale of 1–10 with 1 representing 'Not at all' and 10 representing 'Nearly always', the following statements explore parents' sexual safety rules:

- I/We have clear goals for keeping children and young people safe.
- I/We have made some new rules about keeping children and young people safe.
- Everybody in the family is clear about these rules.
- I/We feel able to make sure that we all stick to the rules.

- I/We can recognise when sexual behaviour is worrying.
- As a family we can draw on the strengths that we have.
- I/We are willing to make some changes if these are needed.
- I/We are able to speak with my/our son/daughter about their behaviour.

The scaled questions enable parents to identify where they are in relation to each statement, provide an opportunity to recognise and convey how they have got to that particular point on the scale and then set achievable and realistic goals for the immediate future that support their movement up the scale and ultimately an increase in safety. Scaled questions are also helpful in safeguarding situations as they encourage truthfulness from the parents as we don't expect them to place themselves at either end of the continuum (and we have found that they rarely do!). Regardless of where they scale themselves it is still possible to talk with them about what needs to be different and specifically what they will be doing differently when they move further up the scale, and what evidence they have for their safety assertions.

Safe care planning is an opportunity to communicate openly about what has happened and what needs to be different for the future. We encourage families to recognise what values are important for them and in particular how they can show respect in their relationships with each other, show age-appropriate responsibilities and allow each other privacy. This is facilitated through whole-family negotiation. Safety is achieved through attention to detail, such as the management of play dates and sleepovers, everyday rules such as safe use of the internet, respect for privacy in bedrooms and bathrooms, and whether or not a baby alarm is needed in the early stages. In addition, the process provides a platform for safety stories to be heard and celebrated. To encourage cooperation and participation we phrase the agreed rules using words and phrases that are future orientated and positive rather than negative, that is, 'will be doing' rather than 'won't be doing'.

Foster children especially need clear rules, routines and expectations, to be kept safe, to know that they are safe and that others are safe from them (Hardwick 2005). For foster carers there is often the issue of safe touching to be decided upon; at the very time when a child needs loving touches, the carer may hesitate to touch them at all in case it triggers a sexual response. Safe touches can be given in the form of safe hugs – from the side, along the shoulders – and safe stroking – gently ruffling a child's hair or stroking the cheek with a fluffy make-up brush. Children are adept at working out how to touch safely; one foster child explained to Judith that a 'Santa Sit' was the safest way to sit on someone's knee – that is, sideways on the knee so there is no danger of private parts coming into contact (Milner 2008).

Once agreed by all family members, the safe home plan is produced and laminated so that the family can display it in the home if they wish (see Figure 5.1, page 113). In addition, signs can be made to remind individual family members to respect privacy in each other's bedrooms.

Safe care plans

Constructing a safe home plan with a family is very much the beginning of the safety process. It provides immediate safeguards but as the responsibility for safety is usually unfairly weighted towards the adults, there are obvious weaknesses. It provides immediate safeguards but as the responsibility of safety, particularly at the beginning, is usually weighted towards the adults, there are obvious weaknesses. It demands minimal responsibility (but which increases over time) on the part of the young person who has harmed others; it only takes one supervising parent to fall ill and the whole plan is in danger of collapsing, and it ignores the need for safety in the wider community. Involvement of wider family and friends is also important as it acts as an extra layer of protection for the vulnerable children in the family. Turnell and Essex (2006) outline the essential elements of an effective safety plan:

1. The dangers must be addressed in clear, straightforward language that is understood by everyone involved. Once these have been identified, the safe care plan is constructed to address these concerns.

'Inappropriate sexual behaviour' is the term most commonly used and we are happy to use it in conversations and feedback notes where it is the term preferred by the young person, but only after the actual behaviours have been spelled out. It is not the term we use when listing our and others' concerns in the safe care plan documentation.

My Safe House

Mum showing trust where I show responsibility

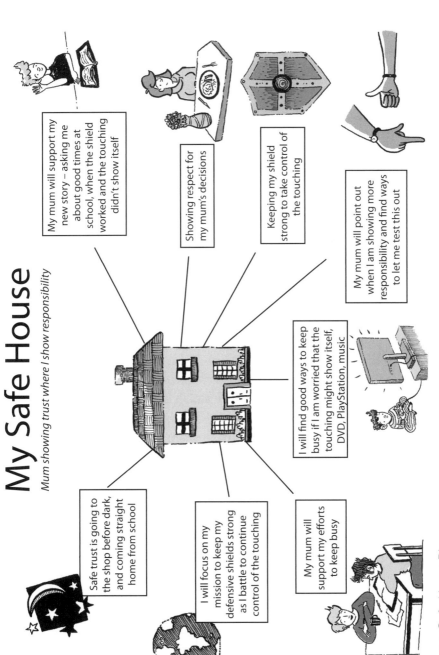

My mum will support my new story – asking me about good times at school, when the shield worked and the touching didn't show itself

Showing respect for my mum's decisions

Keeping my shield strong to take control of the touching

My mum will point out when I am showing more responsibility and find ways to let me test this out

Safe trust is going to the shop before dark, and coming straight home from school

I will focus on my mission to keep my defensive shields strong as I battle to continue control of the touching

My mum will support my efforts to keep busy

I will find good ways to keep busy if I am worried that the touching might show itself, DVD, PlayStation, music

Figure 5.1 Safe Home Plan

✎ **PRACTICE ACTIVITY**

- Consider the case example of Ashley, earlier.
- What concerns do you have about him that will need to be addressed?
- Make a list detailing these concerns.

2. The safe care plan then describes a specific set of detailed behaviours and actions that everyone (parents, family network, and professionals) agrees will demonstrate that the children will be safe from dangers and the offending child safe from further allegations.

Families don't seem to have much difficulty in understanding this process but many professionals find it alien to their ways of thinking and working. The part they find most difficult is identifying exactly what will be happening differently when their current concerns have been allayed. Their goals are often vague – for example, 'He will have an understanding of the impact of his behaviour on other children.' Whilst this is an admirable and desirable goal, it simply isn't measurable. What is important in the construction of the safe care plan is that the specific behaviours that demonstrate safety are identified, that is, exactly what will 'he' be doing differently that will show he understands the impact of his behaviour on others, and how will you measure this.

3. The plan must be developed, refined and implemented successively and over time. It is an ongoing piece of work.

Turnell and Essex (2006) suggest that it takes at least four months for an effective plan to be refined and bedded down. It needs to be sufficiently robust for the family to maintain safety after the professionals withdraw. The process of monitoring provides useful feedback to the family about their successes and opportunities to make changes as circumstances develop. It is only too easy for families to become complacent as the initial problem and accompanying shock fade. When families report a minor slip back, we ask them what they have forgotten to do that was working before. Invariably they report forgetting to do some element of the safety plan.

It also takes time for the young person to take responsibility for their behaviour and make changes to it. It is important that the intervention focuses on this aspect of the safety plan as parents cannot maintain 24/7 vigilance indefinitely. Where the plan is working well, families become more confident to widen their horizons and pick up their lives again. This necessitates changes to the plan to accommodate a holiday or family outings, which may present possible dangers (see the modifications to Kieron's safe care plan when he started going swimming with his brother and family, Chapter 3).

4. It must be endorsed by the statutory authorities involved in the case.

The statutory services need to be as fully engaged as the parents. Working with young people whose behaviour is harmful sexual behaviour is often seen as specialised work but this work must remain embedded in the overall child protection plan. Thus it is worth spending time preparing them for the safety planning process and keeping them fully involved. Where this does not happen, it is not possible to develop an effective safe care plan.

CASE EXAMPLE

Thirteen-year-old Kris has been referred by children's social care following the discovery that he sexually assaulted two boys at his previous school. There are long-standing child protection concerns around neglect but the family social worker says things have improved. Kris has a youth worker. Judith arranged to meet with Kris and his father Mr Smith at home to explain the assessment process and set it in action. She reports:

> This was a spectacularly unproductive meeting. As I walked down the garden path, Kris's brother, Barry, asked me to wait while he took the dogs out. Minutes later he appeared being pulled along by a Rottweiler and a Staffordshire bull terrier. Kris's dad ushered me into the sitting room, where Kris was lounging on a sofa,

engrossed in the television. Mr Smith suggested that it would be better to meet elsewhere as Barry doesn't know all about Kris's behaviour. Neither do the boys get on at all well. Kris's mum is in hospital with an unspecified but recurrent disorder. The house is dirty.

Kris very reluctantly agreed to switch the television off, sign the consent form and go through the referral form. He says he can't remember whether or not the incidents happened but agrees that each incident only happened once. On a scale of 1–10, where 1 is 'what's happening to Kris is not at all serious' and 10 is 'it is so serious it could affect his whole life', Kris rates it at 4 and his dad at 5. Kris considers that all that needs to happen is for it not to happen again – 'Just don't do it, that's it.'

And that is about as far as we got. Kris was pestering his dad for something to eat and Barry returned with the dogs and went into the kitchen. Dad accused Kris of not having his sensible head on and Kris denied having one at all. I briefly outlined the areas of work we will be doing: keeping safe, having safe relationships with kids at his new school, an understanding of the law and consent, good things about Kris and a search for his sensible head.

Kris then joined Barry in the kitchen and the resulting screams demonstrated that the two boys do, indeed, not get on. The dogs and cockatoo joined in the din but the guinea pigs and dad remained quiet.

Judith subsequently met with Kris at his school. He told her that his parents drink approximately two bottles of wine every night. His father continues to do this while his mother is in hospital. He asked that his parents are not told about his disclosure as he fears the consequences, his mother having beaten him up recently. His brother copes with the drunken unpleasantness by getting stoned (cannabis) and then going to bed. Despite them having an alcohol support worker, Kris does not believe that his parents will ever stop drinking. He is a desperately unhappy young person: on a happiness scale, where 1 is as miserable as he could be and 100 is the happiest he could be, he rates himself below 1. On a best person scale, he rates himself at only 28 per cent, indicating that his somewhat cocky presentation is a veneer behind which he hides his misery.

He would like to live with his grandmother, although he knows that this will not be allowed as she is in poor health. He hopes that he could have some sort of shared arrangement whereby he stays with his grandmother for part of the week and the other part in a foster home. He has a sense of responsibility towards his grandmother and shows a capacity for care in this situation.

Kris expressed a willingness to cooperate with an assessment of his sexually concerning behaviour when he is in a situation where he can concentrate on the issues.

Later discussions with his father revealed him to be totally uninterested in working with Kris. The social worker's response was that things had been a lot worse in the family and that she had no intention of bringing the review date forward.

Comment

Kris's sense of responsibility to his grandmother shows that he has some characteristics we look for in building safety. However, he needs to be in a situation that is not only safe but also gives him scope to use these qualities. It is not possible to undertake safe care planning in this situation.

---

5. It must involve everyone in the family and as wide a network as possible.

Turnell and Essex (2006) recommend as wide a network as possible for the safe care plan with a minimum of ten to support the parents and children. Not all families have sufficient extended family members to help out when they are tired or ill, or provide support for the vulnerable children. The Junction developed Helping Teams for this situation, a group of people who come together to encourage and support a young person with the work they need to do to keep themselves and others safe. A Helping Team can include social workers, youth workers, care assistants, teachers, nurses, etc. as well as family members. As well as having specific roles and tasks, they share the important role of ensuring safety.

Young children can be bewildered by events, sometimes misunderstanding what is happening. They still need to be involved in the safety plan in as far as they are capable. Turnell and Essex (2006) recommend using words and pictures as a way of explaining the concerns to children, along with the parents. This process covers the following areas:

- who is worried about the children
- what they are worried about
- what happened then
- private parts
- what family and professionals are doing about the worries.

Attention to the minutiae of the detail is important in safe care planning but it can sometimes lead to a loss of overall focus. We find it helpful to ask ourselves the following questions at regular intervals:

- What are we worried about? (past harm, future danger and complicating factors)
- What's working well? (existing strengths and safety)
- What needs to happen? (future safety)
- Where are we on a scale of 0–10 where 10 means 'there is enough safety to be confident to close the case' and 0 means 'it is certain that a child will be re-abused'?

(Turnell 2012, p.27)

The safe care plan is a formal working document but it doesn't necessarily need to be presented in a solemn format. Whilst it may be a written report or chart, equally it can be a colourful cartoon (see Figure 5.2, page 115).

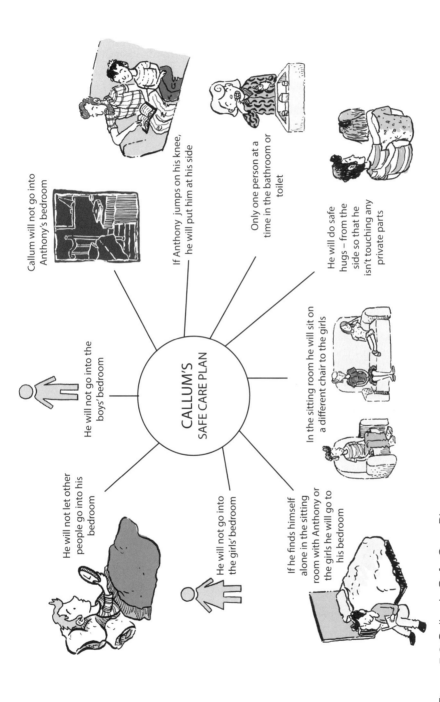

Callum will not go into Anthony's bedroom

If Anthony jumps on his knee, he will put him at his side

Only one person at a time in the bathroom or toilet

He will do safe hugs – from the side so that he isn't touching any private parts

He will not go into the boys' bedroom

In the sitting room he will sit on a different chair to the girls

He will not let other people go into his bedroom

He will not go into the girls' bedroom

If he finds himself alone in the sitting room with Anthony or the girls he will go to his bedroom

CALLUM'S SAFE CARE PLAN

Figure 5.2 Callum's Safe Care Plan

Summary

It is important to involve the family in the process of increasing and maintaining levels of safety. Family members provide insight into how individual members conduct themselves independently, the overall functioning and culture of the family and the values and attitudes that are held. An assessment of parental capacity, willingness and abilities is a necessity and has a significant bearing on levels of safety and whether or not external safeguards are required.

Parents/carers experience a multitude of emotions in response to the realisation that their child has behaved sexually inappropriately. Whilst keeping safety at the centre of the work, professionals need to be sensitive to parental reactions and not be too quick to assess parents as resistant or reluctant to engage. Finding a vocabulary to talk about the behaviour can be difficult at the beginning. The use of externalising, locating and acknowledging the family's strengths and parenting abilities is helpful in this process.

The development of a home safety plan is a vital ingredient to the work. This clarifies rules, boundaries, supervision and responsibilities in and outside of the home. A fully developed safety plan is not a quick fix. It is a robust detailed reflection of what the family will be doing differently in the future, reviewed and amended accordingly to fit ongoing assessed levels of safety.

CHAPTER 6

Working with Young People with Special Needs

Young people with learning difficulties are overrepresented amongst those who sexually harm and require a service. This chapter looks at their special needs and details some specific techniques that are appropriate to their learning styles so that they can increase their understanding and learning in the development of safer behaviours and relationships in the future.

Not surprisingly, the discovery of the over-representation of young people with special needs who sexually harm coincided with the development of group work programmes (Fehrenbach *et al.* 1986; Saunders and Awad 1988; Kahn and Chambers 1991; Day 1993). As Briggs points out, where people are not literate, 'traditional flip-chart work with words to summarise key points within group sessions are of little help' (1994, p.141). This was again reflected a decade later, when Hackett (2004, p.44) reported: 'One of the key changes in the response to adolescent sexual aggression over the past decade is a rapid increase in the number of young people with learning disabilities being identified and referred for intervention.'

Developmental considerations

Although children and young people develop at different rates to each other, there are various behaviours that are considered socially acceptable and appropriate at certain ages and stages of development. For people with special needs their physical/sexual, cognitive, emotional and moral ages are not likely to be smoothly synchronised.

The extent to which this presents a challenge depends largely on the nature of the learning difficulties and the life transitions the young person is experiencing. As with non-sexual offenders, the adolescent sexual offender is often found to be a low achiever, often through a troubled and troublesome childhood (O'Callaghan and Print 1994). Here the issues influencing the focus of the work are largely to do with moral and emotional growth. Where the learning difficulties are linked to a specific condition such as autism, the issues are more likely to involve work on social skill development. Where the young person has profound learning difficulties, the gap between the physical/sexual age and cognitive understanding can be huge.

This has been conceptualised as the young person 'not knowing' what is acceptable and appropriate behaviour due to their learning difficulties. This is both dismissive of the harm that has occurred and also unhelpful to the young person. Regardless of their difficulties, this group of young people will experience sexual urges, thoughts and feelings like any other young person and so require direction in managing these emotions appropriately, both for themselves and others.

 PRACTICE ACTIVITY

Rooney is a well-built 15-year-old lad with profound learning difficulties. As he has no concept of road safety, he travels to his special school by taxi but is due to go to college next term. At school he is supervised closely to prevent him following other pupils into the toilet. At home he plays in the back garden with his best friend, a three-year-old girl who lives next door. Last week he was discovered sucking her toes.

- What are your main concerns and which would you focus on first?
- What are Rooney's needs?

Special needs, sexuality and sexual development

Understanding and learning about sexuality is a process that spans many years. From birth we experience the comfort of being held and cuddled, learn how people interact with each other through observation, gather information through the media and receive both direct and indirect messages about our own and others' bodies being private, the private parts of our bodies, and private and public behaviours and places.

Unfortunately, these conversations are often neglected with young people with special needs or they are simply told 'No' or given negative messages. This can lead to these young people being placed in a vulnerable position – both behaving sexually inappropriately, thus increasing the risk of them being subject to criminal proceedings, particularly as they approach adulthood, as well as their own abuse and exploitation – which sets them apart from their more able contemporaries. Despite this, parents/carers and professionals have often made the assumption that due to a child's special needs, and therefore their 'learning age', their sexual development is not as important. They make the unfortunate decision that participation in any form of sexual education is not required, when in fact it is as important, if not more, because these children are developing sexually but cognitively they are not as developed in their ability to make the right decisions and choices. The denial of their child's sexuality can also impact on how they are socialised with others and they can miss out on natural opportunities to learn the norms of everyday basic social interplay. Young people with learning difficulties need to be provided with the same opportunities to learn and develop their understanding of safe relationships, sexual respect and responsibility and values integral to healthy relationships. The difference is in how these messages and lessons are conveyed and repeated to the young person to increase the likelihood that this important information becomes part of their daily repertoire. Equally, to achieve this, professionals and parents need to be equipped with sufficient understanding and knowledge of the sexual development, sexuality and sexual behaviour of young people with special needs and be confident in their ability to convey the necessary information.

Interventions

When working with a young person with special needs we consider the materials we are going to use, deliver the session at an appropriate pace and make it enjoyable. Basically, we remember to keep sessions relatively brief but hold them more frequently than usual and be conscious of the need for over-learning, with the same material repeated across sessions (Briggs 1994). Over-learning requires the worker to:

- Give frequent reminders and prompts relating to the behaviour that you are working on.

- Talk more slowly and repeat or rephrase important points several times.

- Use pictures or symbols to explain complex concepts such as thoughts and emotions.

- Explain themselves through written or drawn materials as many children find this method of communicating less threatening than face to face conversations.

- Allow time to learn new behaviours so that short chunks of information are repeated several times in fresh ways. Charts and stickers act as useful visual reminders.

- Help the child understand new situations by keeping changes to the minimum.

- Provide opportunities to practise newly learned behaviours.

(Milner and Bateman 2011, p.65)

It is also important to:

- Work in partnership. The work is more effective when professionals work together and establish good means of communication, such as having a home–school diary system in place or joint sessions. (This means that the person who has most contact with the young person can continue the learning during ordinary life.)

- Where possible, use the child's own personal motivations/interests/obsessions to encourage the development of other skills or as a reward for periods of compliance.

- Be sure to state what it is that you want rather than merely saying what you don't want.

(adapted from Speirs undated, pp.4–5)

By remembering these factors, the worker is able to find out how each child or young person learns. There is no set formula for working with young people with special needs; each one will respond best when their unique way of cooperating with you has been determined.

CASE EXAMPLE

Seventeen-year-old Liam is accommodated at a residential home for teenage boys following the attempted rape of a ten-year-old boy. Since coming to live in the home he has made sexual overtures to an especially vulnerable resident, spied on children from his bedroom window and been aggressive to staff (especially women). He is now supervised at all times and has twice weekly one-to-one sessions with his key worker.

The following is a brief extract from the notes of a meeting with Liam, Sharon (his mum), Derek (his key worker), Alan (his social worker) and Judith.

Controlling aggressive responses

Liam continues to be respectful with staff. He is also getting on better with other lads. Before, he couldn't take a laugh and a joke but he can now. He's done this by learning about body and face language. Derek has explained this to Liam.

Liam's mum says that his aggression with his family has been subsiding too. He's not so in her face all the time. Liam's mum explained how very hard it has been for her to take Liam anywhere. She's had to cope with his aggression, keep other kids safe and handle her own feelings. She's been on an emotional roller coaster understanding Liam's behaviour. She couldn't come to terms with who Liam was because it brought up stuff from her past. Seeing Liam as an offender meant he was in her personal space and she had a fear factor. So, even though she loves him to bits, she kept herself safe by cutting herself off from him. It was very helpful for everyone to hear this from Liam's mum; before they hadn't understood how difficult contact was for Sharon.

How Liam learns

Judith and Derek have tried a lot of different ways of explaining things to Liam and it is beginning to look as though charts work best for him. Not reward charts, rather charts that break up each bit of the day and help him to learn routines. Liam's mum explained that she used to put up a long chart with Velcro picture pieces on it to remind him to get up, go to school and stuff like that. Even with this, she had to repeat everything, and she didn't try to tell him stuff that was too far ahead because it wouldn't mean anything to him.

Liam's transition to adult services

Liam will be 18 next birthday so Alan will highlight the support Liam will need and any risks he poses to children. His social worker in adult services and his Connexions worker will still work with Liam when he's transferred to adult services. They may be able to get Liam a place on a life skills programme, or possibly a carpentry skills workshop.

Next steps

1. Because Liam learns through repeated, short-term explanations and with visual reminders, Judith, Derek and Liam will work on a picture chart at their next meeting to cover ordinary routines and safe sex behaviours.

2. Derek will continue the life skills work he has been doing with Liam, and some budgeting.

3. Sharon finds contact with Liam easier when there is a member of staff there too. Maybe she might take Liam out from the home with a member of staff? Or they may stay in. Either way, staff will make sure that she feels safe.

4. Liam has made significant progress in controlling his sexually concerning behaviour so it is important that he's tested in a safe way. A move to a front bedroom would be the simplest

and safest way of testing Liam's progress in controlling his behaviour.

5. Sharon has been coping alone with understanding Liam's behaviour so she will be invited to the parent support group.

Comment

This was the first meeting which Sharon had agreed to attend. Previously residential staff had complained that she showed little interest in Liam, cancelling contact as often as not. Her contribution to the meeting shows a very different picture and highlights the importance of consulting with parents about how best their children learn.

 PRACTICE ACTIVITY

- Remember a successful meeting you had with a child or young person with a learning difficulty.

- Reflect on the way you came to choose this way of communicating.

Specific techniques

Here we outline various techniques which help young people with special needs make sense of which sexual behaviours are acceptable and where. We may try several techniques to find which one fits best with a particular person's learning style. You will have developed techniques of your own for communicating effectively with young people and we encourage you to use them in the context of harmful sexual behaviour – but always with a safety focus.

PRACTICE ACTIVITY

Make a list of all the techniques you use for communicating with children generally. How can these be adapted for work with people with special needs?

CARTOONING

This is especially useful for the young person who struggles with literacy. The visual element of this process enables the young person to create a vision of what could happen in the future and cultivate an increased sense of control over this. A large piece of paper is divided into six squares and the child is invited to draw the problem in the first square, their preferred way of being in the second, who could help them in this process in the third, what could possibly go wrong in the fourth, how this is handled in the fifth, and successes in the sixth (Berg and Steiner 2003).

CASE EXAMPLE

Thirteen-year-old Niamh found it impossible to talk about the 'bottom games' she played with toddlers every time her foster mum's eye was not on her but she found cartooning fun. Her problem square depicted a stick drawing of a sad child, whereas her solution square was more developed. She drew herself wearing jewellery and carrying a handbag, depicting when she was 'more grown up and not doing "that stuff" any more', and her powerful helper was a beautiful angel called Cindy. After this, instead of showing shock and anger when she caught Niamh engaging in sexualised behaviour, her foster carer began asking in a puzzled sort of way, 'Where is Cindy, I thought she was supposed to be helping you?' Very soon, Cindy was around so much that the foster carer was able to buy Niamh her first 'grown up' necklace (Milner 2008).

Cartooning is not just about drawing pictures; it is about helping the young person conceptualise their own problem and work out a solution to it. Therefore, it is not to be rushed and the worker should not worry if the cartoon is not completed. Whatever point the child stops at is the point which needs help and consolidation. It is not unusual for the square showing what the helper will be doing to become the sticking point so it can be useful at this point to draw a helping hand. After the young person has drawn round their hand and written the names or drawn pictures of the people they find helpful, the worker can ask how these people help. Having helped the young person comprehend the concept of helpfulness, the conversation can return to the 'helper' in the drawing. As each concept is mastered, stickers can be awarded.

SCALED QUESTIONS

Due to their versatility and creativity, these are one of the simplest ways of initiating conversations about safer, respectful relationships and reducing feelings of shame and embarrassment. As there are no rigid formats, scales can be completely individualised, encouraging conversations that explore where the young person is in relation to where they have placed themselves on a particular scale. It is important to remember that a person's positioning is unique to them; there is no defined rationale that says you are on a particular point of the scale because you have done a, b or c. Scales could focus on the young person's confidence, understanding and ability in developing appropriate relationships and behaving in safer ways.

As we described them earlier in this book, scales are typically made up of numbers, but they can easily be adapted for a person who struggles with numeracy. A simple ladder scale can be used, or shapes of varying size, so that a young person who may be struggling to communicate verbally can simply choose a shape that represents the size of their problem or a growth (or decrease) in level of confidence, knowledge, etc. We have found that children of all ages and abilities not only enjoy scaled questions but sometimes create their own versions. One young man drew Judith a picture of his temper that had a coloured stripe on one side. He explained that the deep purple at the top was his bad temper and the paler colours at the bottom were his 'calm'. Without prompting, he located himself on the pinkish purple stripe ladder (Milner and Bateman 2011, p.20).

When talking about healthy relationships, a young person with special needs could be asked to identify someone they know or television characters who they identify as behaving in appropriate and inappropriate ways. These characters can then become either end of the scale. You could explore what the characters do that makes their behaviour appropriate or inappropriate and then ask the young person where they position themselves on the scale in relation to these two characters. Whichever representation is used (numbers, shapes, characters, pictures) once the young person has identified where they are on a particular scale you would then enquire what they have done that warrants a particular positioning. The next steps would be to consider what else needs to be happening in their lives to move further up the scale and – as we have found, particularly with young people with special needs – how important it is to identify what others need to be doing to support this venture. Ultimately, it will result in the young person and their parents/carers identifying with ideas and rules that they have found work for them.

 PRACTICE ACTIVITY

Consider the three scaled questions below:

- On a scale of 1–10, where would you say you are in understanding what OK behaviours look like?

- On a scale of 1–10, how confident are you in recognising signs that someone fancies you?

- On a scale of 1–10, how confident are you in showing that you fancy someone in an appropriate way?

Changing either the numbers or words – or both – redesign these questions so that they would be comprehensible to a young person with special needs with whom you have been working.

Once you have designed scaled questions to fit the young person's level of understanding and learning style, you can then decide on supplementary questions to assess whether the everyday ideas and concepts that are being discussed are being translated and replicated in their daily behaviour and routines:

- Tell me when you did this.
- Have other people noticed this?
- What did this look like?
- Where were you?
- Who were you with?

Supplementary questions help the young person recognise times when they have behaved in safer ways.

MR MEN CHARACTERS

We devised an extension of the Mr Men characters for conversations with children and young people whose special needs are profound, only to discover that most young people like them. They have the advantage of being easy to draw, needing no more than a circle or square for the body and lines drawn for arms and legs, plus a defining characteristic. The defining characteristic is the name the child has chosen for the problem – for example, Mr Touchy. Or you might use a blank Mr Men figure so that the young person can name him – or her. More than one young person has chosen 'Mr Just Do It'. This enables you to ask for exceptions to the problem behaviour: 'Tell me about a time when Mr Just Do It tried to get you into trouble but you took no notice of him?' Or you could invite the young person to describe the opposite Mr Men character and then use the two characters at either end of a scale.

MAPS AND CHARTS

As an alternative to worksheets we have used charts and maps. These are creative tools which help the child to visualise where they are in relation to a particular quest. They also highlight and reinforce expectations and create consistency and document achievements. For example, Jackie worked with Paul who had been placed approximately

100 miles away from home after inappropriately touching his seven-year-old sister on several occasions. Jackie met with Paul on a regular basis and at the end of each session they would look at a road map which detailed the journey from his current placement to home and equate the current levels of safety to where he was on the map. Like a scaling exercise the conversation would focus on what Paul had been doing to warrant his 'arrival' at a particular destination, as well as what was required for Paul to cover the next 10 miles and/or town.

A chart was used with Tom, a 12-year-old boy, to capture his achievements in showing 12-year-old Responsibility. Tom's overarching goal was to achieve a silver certificate in 'practising privacy'. He identified three ways that he was going to demonstrate this: shutting his bedroom door when he wanted to masturbate, dressing with his curtains shut and safer touching. From a selection of stickers he identified one for each of his safer behaviours and then at the end of each day added a sticker to his chart if he achieved 'practise privacy' in one or all identified ways. Jackie has also used world maps where the young person can do some 'globe-trotting' across their chosen countries, with each country signifying a particular improvement and progress in behaving (sexually) more appropriately.

Judith uses a simple combination of maps and charts where she draws two roads with a fork, with one fork leading to the desired safety (and the young person's goal) and the other leading to danger (and the possible consequences for the young person of taking that route). The young person adds to the illustration with colouring and pictures and words, depending on their level of ability. Depicting their situation in this pictorial manner enables the young person to appreciate the effects of their actions and helps them become future focused.

CASE EXAMPLE

How these techniques can be woven together to facilitate solution finding to a serious slip back on the part of 13-year-old David is illustrated by an extract below from the notes shared with the family after session seven. David's permanent placement was threatened after his prospective foster carer Christine found that he had taken her knickers, and her ten-year-old daughter's, and stuffed them behind the bathroom washbasin during a weekend visit. As they were stained, it was obvious that David had masturbated over them. The session described below included David, the carers Christine and Ron and their two children Lucy and Andrew, and Judith. David was functioning academically at about the level of a seven-year-old but, although steadily improving, his social skills were much more rudimentary.

Notes of meeting to discuss David's slip back

On discovery, Christine had told David that she was shocked and upset and that he wouldn't be coming to live with her if he continued to do such things. David's face quivered and this was the first strong emotional response that David had shown. As David tends to lie about serious issues, Judith re-visited the earlier work on respect so that the knicker episode could be raised in the context of wider issues to do with respectfulness towards women.

Each child was asked what they had done recently that had gone well. This was elaborated (how did they do this?) and celebrated before they were asked what had not gone well. Lucy reported herself for staying out later than she had been told; Andrew for being 'lippy' (but not as bad as he used to be); and David for barging into people on a recent holiday in his haste to get where he was going. Christine also reminded him of the knicker episode and that knickers are private, wherever they are, as they cover private parts (reminding him of material discussed in a previous session).

Judith asked the children to draw a picture of a road with two forks – the right road to respect and the wrong road. As David has difficulty writing words, he coloured his two roads red (wrong road) and green (right road). They were then asked to give an example of respectful behaviour: Lucy said people knocking on her bedroom before entering; Andrew said giving borrowed things back, and giving them back in the condition received; and David said having manners and not barging. We then looked at how grown-ups do respect. Lucy said that mum shows respect by cooking for them, getting their clothes ready and stuff like that. Andrew said that dad shows respect by going to work and providing for them – everyday stuff and holidays. David couldn't think of any way in which Christine and Ron show him respect so he was reminded about what they are doing to provide him with a home. Judith explained to the children that grown-ups show respect for children even when they are tired but that children are still learning and don't always remember to do respect; that grown-ups have to remind them; and that there are consequences for disrespectful behaviour.

She then asked what happened when they had been disrespectful. Andrew said he got grounded or his Xbox taken away; Lucy said told off or grounded; and David couldn't think of any consequences. Judith asked him if he knew what a sanction was and he worked out that it's what happens after disrespect (at his temporary foster home he gets sent to his bedroom). Christine had tended to show disappointment when David was disrespectful as this works with Lucy and Andrew but it doesn't work well with David. David agreed that a sanction for any disrespect on his part should be that he is not allowed on the computer and has to tidy up his clothes instead. The children were clear about consequences for grown-ups who are not respectful – David made the link with his birth parents not being allowed to look after children after they had done things that were sexually disrespectful.

They each drew a Mr Men type figure of their disrespect. Andrew drew a Mr Lippy with a big mouth, Lucy drew a Mr Please Myself and David drew a Mr Just Do It. We talked about how these Mr Men took them on the wrong road and what happened if they went down the wrong road – sanctions and lack of freedom (developing David's road map). Then they drew a Mr Men figure to help them stay on the right road. Andrew drew a Mr Zip Gob, Lucy a Mr Watch and David a Mr Think.

At the following session, David's behaviour had improved all round. There were no problems with sexually concerning behaviour and David proudly reported that he had told no lies for a week. He had done this by using his 'thinking' (his adaptation of Mr Think). Particularly striking was his intellectual and social progress; David was beginning to understand the concepts involved in respectfulness and truthfulness, could handle complexity and was much more open and chatty. His relationship with Ron had strengthened too; it was noticeable how they exchanged knowing smiles and were relaxed and comfortable with each other. It is important to make male carers' roles explicit as they are especially liable to be sidelined as a result of fear of false allegations being made (Hardwick 2005).

SOCIAL STORIES

We use social stories (Gray 1991) as a helpful addition to reinforce the messages and/or rules that have been discussed in family sessions. Social stories originated as a creative way of working with children and young people who were assessed as being on the autistic spectrum (Gray 1991). They have also been used with children with special needs (Reynhout and Carter 2006). The stories consist of sets of written statements about a type of behaviour, event or situation with which a young person may be presently struggling. Traditionally, social stories consider how someone should and should not be behaving. However, Jackie has adapted them so that the context of the story is always focused on what will be happening and so remaining within a safety framework. Furthermore, the young person is involved in the writing process. Like safety plans, discussed in the previous chapter, these stories can then be laminated and displayed in the home or carried around by the young person. Judith also uses them to help the young person think ahead, but adds a similar but different character so that the young person is talking about another person doing what they did, or what they could do instead. She begins a story and then it develops as they take turns to write a sentence, so it becomes a relatively unthreatening way of having a conversation.

CASE EXAMPLE

Fifteen-year-old Gavin does not like talking about his harmful sexual behaviour – or his vulnerability to sexual exploitation – and he especially dislikes eye contact, so all the work done with him took the form of drawing, cards or writing stories. He chose a character for himself called Phil and wrote the story on the following page about how Phil learned the hard way about the dangers of getting into a car with a stranger.

As with all young people, but particularly young people with special needs, there is no quick fix to their understanding and appreciation of the intricate rules of social interaction. Regular reinforcement is required and this is best done by the people who live with the young person. As can be seen in the examples of Liam and David (previously) it pays dividends to include parents, carers and their children (they need to be kept safe too), and any other professionals involved with the young person, such as youth workers. As part of the action plan they can ensure that messages of appropriate behaviours are reinforced on a daily basis and then replicated in the young person's social interaction with others. Including parents, carers and others in the action plan also increases their skills in recognising and responding to sexualised behaviour appropriately, increases their confidence and ability and therefore the likelihood that professional intervention is not required on a long-term basis.

It is easy to forget that having special needs does not mean the young person can't do anything. As with any other child or young person, it is important to discover what strengths and resources they already possess. It is even more important to link any existing strengths in respectful and caring behaviours to your learning exercises. For example, Rooney (see earlier) was able to care for his two guinea pigs with a little reminder.

Phil was playing on the road this bad man came up to him he asked Phil to show him where the pub was this man had a nice smile is this did not Phil not the he was a bad man Phil said no because he new not to go with strangers the man smiled again good he said show me where the pub is and i give you a siver Phil said ok and went to the pub with the man o Dear said the man ive just remembered all my money is at home jump in my car and we will go and get your siver Phil gets in the car with the man and the man drives of but he doesnt go to his house he drives out onto a lonely hill the man isnt smiling anymore Phil is getting very worried he doesnt even know where he is he thinks his mum would be worrying to about him give the siver and drive me home the man stops the car stop morning and earn your siver he says take your trousers DOWN Phil jos out of the car Phil has run away as fast as he could the bad man was too fat to chase him Phil has ran and ran and ran and till he saw some walkers he new the walkers that they please please more because they were sow of them a men walking help me so they taken me home on the bus to my mum his mum give every one accosted and then she rang the Police about the badman Phil never got the siver

Phil nows not to get into cars with strangers for a siver

PRACTICE ACTIVITY

- Think of a child or young person you find challenging and/or frustrating.
- Now think of three good things about this person.
- Ask his/her carers what good things they have noticed.
- What questions can you ask the child or young person that will reveal these things to them?
- How can you use these qualities to develop your work with this child or young person?

Summary

Young people with learning difficulties are over-represented in referrals to services working with sexually problematic behaviour. It is helpful to provide appropriate opportunities for this group of young people to develop their understanding of the components of a healthy relationship regardless of cognitive impairment.

Safety work with young people with learning difficulties needs to consider the way in which they learn best, being mindful of the structure of the session, what the session will look like and how this information will be delivered. Regular reinforcement of any new learning in the young person's daily regime aids safety development. This reinforcement is best done by the people with whom the young person lives and is a reminder of the necessity to include parents and carers within the work.

Often the young person's disability can take precedence and their resources and abilities are forgotten, so a focus on recognising a young person's strengths and skills can be useful in increasing future safety.

CHAPTER 7

Working in Schools

This chapter addresses ways in which problematic sexual behaviour can be addressed in schools to maintain the safety of students and avoid excluding pupils. The three elements of a whole-school approach are described and illustrated: engaging with a class as a whole on what constitutes a 'safe classroom' and how this can be developed and maintained, developing individual safety plans and teaching protective behaviours.

Much of what has been described in Chapter 5 on working with families applies here; it is the larger context that demands more coordination of effort. For example, there is usually a question of who needs to know? Obviously not every single person in the school environment needs to know about one child's sexually concerning behaviour, but the people who are the key to other people's safety do need to know where they fit into the safety plan. And often concerns about the behaviour arise in school so school staff all need to know how to respond. Although there may be a named teacher with specific responsibility for dealing with pupils with sexually concerning behaviour, all school staff will want to be confident in recognising and responding to sexualised behaviour.

There are no specific figures which highlight the extent of this issue in schools, although research by NSPCC (2013) would recognise schools as a contributing referral source. Our own working experience and contact with schools over the last ten years supports the view that this behaviour continues to be a problem and that staff welcome support in managing this. Part of schools' difficulty in recognising and responding to sexualised behaviour in schools is difficulty 'in distinguishing between normal childhood sexual development and experimentation, and sexually inappropriate or aggressive behaviour' (HM Government 2010, p.304). They need to be confident and skilled in responding to sexualised behaviour to ensure the safety of all concerned. As young people spend a significant amount of their time in schools, schools are in a strong position to be able to identify inappropriate behaviours and influence their pupils' sexual as well as personal development and therefore have a significant part to play when any problematic sexual behaviours have occurred. This is especially true of residential schools.

 PRACTICE ACTIVITY

Nine-year-old Emma is experiencing difficulties at school and her parents are finding it hard to get her to attend. She sometimes leaves school at midday. She has previously been reprimanded for playing games with younger children that involve her in taking their knickers down. Yesterday she was seen disappearing into the bushes at the edge of the playground with a male classmate.

- What are the issues here?
- Who would be best placed to talk to Emma first?
- How would you talk to Emma?
- Do you need to talk to the other children too?

(adapted from Myers and Milner 2007, p.69)

Recognising and responding

As we highlighted in previous chapters, for some adults thinking and talking about children's sexual behaviour generates feelings of discomfort, embarrassment and confusion and this can extend to teaching staff, affecting how they respond to the behaviour. The appropriateness of their response can also be influenced by their understanding of what constitutes appropriate sexual behaviour as well as the myths and misconceptions about this group of young people.

School staff require support to address both their feelings and special needs relating to this subject area so that they become confident in supporting young people with problematic sexual behaviour whilst still ensuring the safety of others and the prevention of sexually inappropriate behaviour in the school.

Recognising and responding to sexually inappropriate behaviour assumes an understanding of the difference between expected, concerning and harmful sexual behaviours. The practical way of beginning to understand the differences by considering a sexual behaviour continuum described in Chapter 5 is relevant here, although the scenarios need to be amended to reflect the school context; for example:

- Stephen, 11 years old, has been sending pictures of his penis by phone to girls in his class.

- Sally, six years old, and her friend Karen, also six years old, were found in the school playhouse looking at each other's vulva.

- Alex, nine years old, would repeatedly look under the toilet doors when they were occupied and touched his teacher's breasts on several occasions.

- Robert, 15 years old, pushed a 12-year-old girl to the ground on the sports field, pulled her shirt up, sucked her breast and attempted to pull her knickers down.

Where do these behaviours fit on the sexual behaviour continuum? Do the young people have equal power and an ability to consent? Was force or coercion used?

Inevitably there will be specific procedures to follow through the school's child protection policy and schools should be active partners in the support of any investigations and then contributors to any future plans and risk management processes. At the same time, despite the recommendations regarding agencies working together, schools are often left to manage the aftermath independently of any specific direction. Schools have to juggle both the needs of the young person who has been sexually abusive as well as those young people who may have been affected, both directly and/or indirectly through witnessing. Schools also need to manage and respond sensitively to parents of all parties whose reactions can range from outrage to denial, embarrassment and shame.

A further strand to consider is when the behaviour has occurred outside school premises. Home–school safety plans need to consider the safety needs of other children at after school clubs, youth clubs and sports clubs. And there is the all-important issue of who is responsible for safety when the young person is travelling between home and school. The best-devised safety plan will fail if this vulnerable environment is ignored.

Safety planning

The basic premise of a school safety plan (see Figure 7.1 on page 142) is similar to that of a safe home plan with the obvious difference that it is within the context of a school environment. The framework/process of the plan should support the young person in taking responsibility for their behaviour without shaming or pathologising them or condoning and minimising the impact of their behaviour. Sometimes when young people have behaved inappropriately, whether this is sexual or non-sexual, the adults in their lives have made the decision about how this is to be managed and responded to without any consultation with the young person. We would argue that for young people to achieve increased independence and responsibility for their behaviour and future safety and to be able to sustain any changes that are made they need to be considered as strategic partners in any management plan.

The construction of an individual school safety plan should be one of collaboration between relevant agencies, the school, the young person and their carers/parents to assess and develop safety. A robust plan will reflect the context of the behaviour, taking into account the frequency, number of 'victims', location of behaviour and level/seriousness of the behaviour. For example, a small child who has regularly masturbated in class will have a different safety plan to a young person who has coerced a younger child to touch his penis in the toilet on a number of occasions. Other considerations for the plan may be levels of supervision within structured and unstructured periods; alternative venues for break times; checking in with other staff such as learning mentors over longer lunch breaks and at the beginning and end of school; and identifying a person who the young person can approach at any time if they are experiencing difficulties. Alternative or additional lessons may also be a useful addition to a young person's timetable, covering some of the subject areas referred to earlier in the chapter. It is equally important that a young person's level of supervision is not so extreme that they are unable to engage in any peer activities. Such activities provide opportunities for a young person to observe and develop appropriate social interaction with others. Finally, the safety process should also include reviews of the plan to assess ongoing levels of safety, as well as the young person's strengths and capabilities. These forums provide opportunities for all parties to provide evidence that either levels of safety have increased and therefore a reduction in supervision is warranted, or alternatively that a young person has struggled to abide by the agreements and other restrictions are required.

CASE EXAMPLE

Richard, 12 years old, had exposed his penis on several occasions in the playground. Girls have complained that they feel uncomfortable when he gets too close to them. Richard also rubs his genital area over his clothes.

An individual school safety plan was developed with Richard that addressed the safeguarding needs of other young people and gave age-appropriate responsibility to Richard, whilst providing him with sufficient support. The following 'rules' were agreed by all:

- Richard's lunch times to begin five minutes later and end five minutes earlier. (This addressed his anxiety that became apparent with the chaos that occurred at the beginning and end of the lunch period when there was so much movement within the school environment.)

- A learning mentor to be assigned and Richard to go to her room when he arrives at school and break times (as an alternative to going into the playground).

- During the lunch period Richard to remain in the lower part of the playground within view of the playgroup supervisor.

- Richard to do some individual work with his learning mentor about personal space. His teachers to notice when Richard is practising this and tell him at the end of each lesson.

John's
Safe School Plan

John is part of a group of 5 boys who meet at lunchtimes to… GET THINGS SORTED!

There will be a celebration after 6 of these meetings

If John feels wobbly and thinks he might choose NOT OK BEHAVIOUR, or if "The Touching Problem" is nearby, he will speak to a teacher and show his "TIME OUT" card

He can chill out on the landing or in the book corner till he has calmed down

We all want John to do well, make friends and…

…have a successful move to comprehensive school

Teachers like to see that John is showing OK behaviour by him…

- getting spellings right
- doing his reading
- keeping to school rules
- doing homework
  (and remembering diary)

If John chooses to show these GOOD BEHAVIOURS he can…

- get stamps in his diary
- earn team points
- receive certificates
- 3 certificates = bowling and Pizza Hut with Mum

Teachers have noticed that John…

- is open and honest
- helps do jobs for the dinner ladies
- speaks in a calm way and is growing up
- says please and thank you
- can now remember to put his hand up
  (and NOT shout!)

Figure 7.1 John's Safe School Plan

PRACTICE ACTIVITY

- Which staff members need to know about the plan for Richard?
- What do they need to know?
- What observations should they make?
- To whom should they report their observations?

Interventions
INDIVIDUAL SAFETY PLANS

Traditionally, the school environment has been considered to be problem focused in that it was orientated to what a child can't do and/ or their mistakes. However, the school environment has huge potential for applying a strengths-based approach and focusing on a child's skills and achievements with the goal of increasing competences in those areas where a student may be struggling. This can include behaving in more socially appropriate ways. It also provides increased levels of confidence and motivation in increasing the virtuous behaviours that others would like to see demonstrated. Teachers, learning assistants and mentors can act as detectives in a young person's life, documenting changes and improvements, however small, and feeding back to the young person and others. When behaviour deteriorates they can consider what needs to be different to build upon the positive changes to increase safety.

CASE EXAMPLE

Susan, 12 years old, was regularly masturbating in the classroom and occasionally taking her top off and exposing her breasts. A safety plan was developed with Susan and in addition Susan carried a positive comments book around with her. During each day teachers, lunchtime supervisors and her learning mentor could note and reflect on any behaviours that evidenced respectful, responsible and safer behaviours. This worked well for several weeks, to the point where Susan stopped exposing herself and masturbated much less frequently. However, Susan wasn't able to maintain these improvements on a longer-term basis and began exposing herself again. There was puzzlement about why this was happening. Jackie and Susan looked through her positive comments book and noticed that there were numerous occasions when Susan's improved behaviour had resulted in her being given little jobs of responsibility. However, whilst positive comments had continued these tasks had not. When consulting with Susan she confirmed that she had felt 'grown up' when given some extra responsibilities and that 'grown-ups didn't show their private parts'. It was agreed that increased levels of responsibility would be given to Susan incrementally to reflect her 'grown up' behaviour. Seven months later Susan's behaviour was no longer sexually concerning and she had achieved her goal of being part of the school's 'buddy' system for new pupils.

SAFE CLASSROOMS

Conversations about behaving safely and appropriately and how young people demonstrate these behaviours to each other should be considered as part of the ethos of the school and not necessarily isolated instruction in PHSE or in response to any concerning behaviour that has occurred. Jackie has worked with schools, increasing levels of respect and safer behaviour in classrooms and schools as a whole. Adopting a strengths approach Jackie would enquire with the class about their goals by asking questions such as:

- What makes a safe classroom?
- What does a safe classroom look like?
- How is this experienced in this classroom?
- How is everyone behaving?
- How do you demonstrate appropriate behaviours with each other?

Part of the process includes the students interviewing each other about their individual and group strengths, which can be used to support the introduction and maintenance of a safer classroom. Scenarios which could unbalance the equilibrium of the safer classroom are proposed to test these strengths and identify class solutions to such situations.

- How can you help someone if they need help to remember what is OK and not OK in your safe classroom?

- If someone is upsetting you how can you tell them in a helpful way? Who else can you call upon?

Once there is a clear and concrete understanding of their hopes and what the safer classroom looks like, Jackie will enquire about the exceptions to the unsafe behaviour. For example, when students highlight that a safer classroom would be where there is no inappropriate touching, Jackie would ask:

- When there is no inappropriate touching happening, how are people behaving instead?

- Can you tell me about times when this is already happening?

- What was different on these occasions?

- Who was around?

Recognising these alternative times can be an empowering and motivating experience, for both the teacher and young people. The final part of the process is the production of the safe classroom plan.

- What else needs to be happening so that more of this safer behaviour is happening within your classroom?

- What do you need to be doing more of to build upon the safety that is already happening?

At this point the class begins to identify their 'rules' and a safety plan is developed.

Figure 7.2 Rules for a Safe Classroom

The safer classroom work can be adapted to reflect a variety of ages and be undertaken with the whole class. It is envisaged that such an exercise will open up communication about personal space and boundaries, how people communicate with each other, being in control of one's own body, distinguishing between appropriate and inappropriate touch and how to respond to an inappropriate touch.

Constructing questions which are future orientated provides opportunities for young people to begin to imagine what something could actually be like. For example, again considering the context of increased safety within a classroom, a question such as the following could be posed: 'Imagine that at the end of the day you are ask to scale the safety levels of your classroom and you decide upon a 9.5, what has been happening throughout the day to warrant this scale?' This can be done on a micro level (classroom) or macro level (the whole school). The point of the process is to provide a reflective space for young people (and staff) to consider and construct what a safer classroom/school could look like. Similarly, scales could be used to provide a platform for young people to assess safety levels again within their class and school. Either will lead to further conversations about where these behaviours have already been witnessed or experienced (exceptions). By providing opportunities to examine what was different opens up possibilities and ideas for what to do next.

PROTECTIVE BEHAVIOURS

As well as safe classroom work another approach that can be incorporated into the school ethos and practice as well as individually in the classrooms is the promotion of protective behaviours learning. The overarching goal of this programme is to increase an individual's understanding of what safety is by differentiating between safe, unsafe and risky situations. It also aims to increase levels of confidence and assertiveness to feeling and being safe. A protective behaviours programme is framed within two key messages: an individual's right to feel safe and the encouragement to talk about something regardless of its size and how bad it is.

It is a very practical programme that helps children and young people (and adults) to identify situations where they feel unsafe by recognising their body's early warning signs. Children can draw around each other so that they have a template of the body or simply draw an outline of the body and then discuss the different parts of the body and how these parts react to safe and unsafe feelings. This could also extend to learning about and practising use of the correct anatomical names for body parts as well as understanding about the public and private parts of the body. This learning can then be reinforced through a school assembly, maybe through the reading of a story that considers the physical and emotional signs that we notice when we don't feel safe or a question and answer session that captures these themes. Identifying and developing a support network and thinking about rights and responsibilities is also part of the protective behaviours process.

There are criticisms of formalised protective behaviours teaching. The biggest drawback is that it treats the subject as a specialised expertise in which teachers require training at different levels. This automatically deskills school staff, many of whom probably have a good understanding of how to explain about protective behaviours via their own parenting experiences. We are also concerned about asking children to lie down and have an outline of their body drawn; for many children this is itself intrusive and probably a request that a child with confidence in their ability to say no would promptly refuse. And while even young children can grasp the concepts of sexual safety training they still find it difficult to say no or tell when faced with a persuasive or powerful adult. Children with physical and learning difficulties are especially vulnerable to sexual abuse, and their carers have been found consistently to over-estimate their charges' understanding (Banat, Summers and Pring 2002). Research shows that children are more likely to act on their knowledge if they have problem-solving skills. Elliott (1985) suggests that 'what if?' games are a playful way of improving a child's problem-solving skills. She recommends that the 'what if?' questions start with something simple, like 'What if a monkey came to the door?' and follow this with more general safety questions, such as 'What if you saw smoke coming from the house next door?' before moving on to more sensitive questions, such as 'What if your babysitter offered to let you stay up late if you play secret games?'

Keeping-safe teaching can be supported in lots of simple ways, such as careful selection of reading material. For example, a storybook such as *Jezebel* makes the point in a humorous way that over-compliance in children can be dangerous. Establishing a child's right to feel and be safe can be supported by talking about rights and safety in an incremental way. For example, you could ask children about basic rights such as breathing, eating, sleeping and going to the toilet, and what would happen if these rights were taken away. Then introduce the idea of the right to feel safe by asking the child for examples of when they feel safe. Before talking about body safety, it is useful to ask about other safety situations, such as does the child know how to keep safe in the home (around scissors and knives, for example), on the road, if lost, and so on. As each safety competency is established it can then be recorded on the individual child's safety log. For a fuller description of sexual safety training for children and young people, see Myers and Milner 2007, Chapter 5.

 PRACTICE ACTIVITY

Ten-year-old Michael and his nine-year-old sister Sadie have been sexually abused by a family friend. They both attend their local junior school, although Michael has a statement of special educational needs, since he has been diagnosed with Asperger's syndrome (from September 2014 these statements have been replaced with education, health and care plans). Sadie is showing similar traits. Michael has a reading age of seven but does not always comprehend what he has read. Sadie has a reading age of five. They are both very eager to please and have no concept of sexual safety.

- How would you approach keep safe work with these children?
- Which materials might be useful?

(adapted from Myers and Milner 2007, p.74)

Internet safety

Whilst we recognise that families have the primary role as educators in their child's life, taking into account the period of time a child is part of the educational environment, schools also play a crucial role in supporting and influencing young people to adopt appropriate behaviours and encourage healthy decision making as they navigate through what can be a tricky and unsettling period of life. Traditionally, the Personal, Social and Health Education (PSHE) curriculum has been the main, if not only, opportunity for young people to be taught about relationships and appropriate behaviours. Whilst we wouldn't discourage this we would argue that other forums and opportunities could be seized within the school environment, for example, circle time for primary age children and assembly or class presentations and role play for older students. In addition we would argue for thoroughness and attention to detail in these discussions so that young people are grounded in what constitutes consent, respect and responsibility, an appreciation of their own and others' bodies, values and attitudes, appropriate and safe touching and behaviours, and the development and negotiation involved in healthy relationships. Inevitably, these conversations will need to be age appropriate to the audience both in terms of content and delivery. We have also found that the use of board games, cards, puppets and books are useful in exploring all these areas.

In the ever-developing arena of digital technology, there can be a fine balance between the learning benefits of this genre and the safeguarding implications. In recognition of the concerns highlighted in the report *'Basically… Porn is Everywhere'* (Horvath *et al.* 2013) and the impact that inappropriate material can have on a young person's attitude to sex and relationships, it is imperative that schools are equipped to manage and respond to the ever-growing phenomena of the digital world. One of the themes that stood out in Byron's review (2008) was the potential role that schools (and other children's services) have in delivering e-safety support and learning to children and young people. In relation to schools there were a number of recommendations including:

- that e-safety best practice is well reflected in guidance and exemplar case studies across the curriculum as part of the support being provided to help schools to implement the new curriculum (p.129)

- [a] focus on e-safety by identifying it as a national priority for the continuous professional development (p.130)

- action taken at a whole-school level to ensure that e-safety is mainstreamed throughout the school's teaching, learning and other practices. (p.132)

Equally, we are recognising that the promotion of child safety involves more than adults simply keeping children safe from potentially risky situations and people. Adults are, in any event, not always in the best position to do this because children are often more knowledgeable than their parents about digital media. Whilst adults are needed to create a safe environment, children and young people need to be equipped with knowledge to enable them to make the right choices about keeping themselves safe. This growth in autonomy was highlighted in Ofsted's report *The Safe Use of New Technologies* (2010) with schools using 'managed' rather than 'locked down' systems, concurring with Byron's second review which reported that:

> simply blocking children and young people's access to the internet in schools…meant that they weren't able to access a range of sites that were beneficial for learning, and that they were less likely to develop the understanding of digital safety that they needed to be digitally safe outside of school. (Byron 2010, p.16)

The report also concurred with reflections in the review by Dr Linda Papadopoulos *Sexualisation of Young People* (2010) that digital safety should not be restricted to a single subject but is best approached on a whole-school level and integrated throughout the curriculum.

Two years on, similar issues were reflected in the article 'Empower, engage, encourage, enable: how to keep pupils safe online' where Bower (2012) states 'schools must move towards embedding e-safety within the curriculum, providing a progression for its learners, where the technology is used to enhance learning and children recognise risk and understand the need for safety and responsibility' (p.6). In addition, Ofsted's (then) new inspection framework included a criterion on e-safety, assessing how well schools were protecting pupils from being bullied and encouraging safe, respectful and considerate behaviours towards others when engaging online, all of which can begin to be challenged through appropriate e-safety teaching.

Summary

Schools play a significant role in identifying and influencing a young person's sexual behaviour. The management of sexualised behaviour in schools is best approached on a whole-school as well as classroom/ curriculum and individual level so that children are taught how to protect themselves and school staff become confident in recognising and responding to sexualised behaviour.

Not every person in the school environment needs to be aware of an individual's harmful sexual behaviour but significant people, such as form teachers or learning mentors, need to be actively involved in the planning process to increase the safety of all concerned and contribute towards the prevention of sexually inappropriate behaviour in the school. The school, young person, parents/carers and any relevant agencies should be fully involved in the production of the safety plan. The safety plan should reflect the context of the behaviour whilst not being so restrictive that it limits opportunities for the young person to engage in peer activities and develop appropriate social interaction within the school environment.

Communication on safe and healthy sexual relationships and appropriate sexual behaviours and general sexual education need not be restricted to PSHE lessons but should be incorporated within the ethos and practices of the classes and school as a whole.

REFERENCES

Alexander, M.A. (1999) 'Sexual offender treatment efficacy revisited.' *Sexual Abuse: A Journal of Research and Treatment 11*, 101–116.

Audit Commission (1998) *Misspent Youth 98: The Challenge for Youth Justice*. London, UK: Audit Commission Publications.

Augusta-Scott, T. (2007) 'Letters from Prison: Re-authoring Identity with Men Who Have Perpetrated Sexual Violence.' In C. Brown, and T. Augusta-Scott (eds) *Narrative Therapy: Making Meaning, Making Lives*. London, UK: Sage.

Banat, D., Summers, S., and Pring, T. (2002) 'An investigation into carers' perceptions of the verbal comprehension ability of adults with a learning disability.' *British Journal of Learning Disabilities 30*, 2, 78–81.

Barnado's (2005) *Safe Care: A Guide for Parents of Children who Sexually Offend*. Rotherham, UK: Barnado's The Junction.

Bateman, J. and White, N. (2008) 'The use of narrative therapy to allow the emergence of engagement.' *International Journal of Narrative Therapy and Community Work 2*, 17–28.

Berg, I.K. and Reuss, N.H. (1998) *Solutions, Step by Step: A Substance Abuse Treatment Manual*. New York, NY: W.W. Norton.

Berg, I.K. and Steiner, T. (2003) *Children's Solution Work*. London, UK: W.W. Norton.

Bird, J. (2000) *The Heart's Narrative: Therapy and Navigating Life's Contradictions*. Auckland, Australia: Edge Press.

Briggs, D. (1994) 'The Management of Sex Offenders in Institutions.' In T. Morrison, M. Erooga and R.C. Beckett (eds) *Sexual Offending Against Children: Assessment and Treatment of Male Abusers*. London, UK: Routledge.

Brindle, N., Branton, T., Stansfield, A. and Zigmond, T. (2013) *A Clinician's Brief Guide to the Mental Capacity Act*. London, UK: RCPsych Publications.

Byron, T. (2008) *Safer Children in a Digital World: Report of the Byron Review*. London, UK: DCSF and DCMS.

Byron, T. (2010) *Do We Have Safer Children in a Digital World? Review of Progress since the 2008 Byron Review*. Nottingham, UK: DCSF.

Caldwell, M.F. (2002) 'What we do not know about juvenile sexual re-offense risk.' *Child Maltreatment 7*, 4, 291–302.

Caldwell, M.F (2007) 'Sexual offense adjudication and sexual recidivism among juvenile offenders,' *Sexual Abuse: A Journal of Research and Treatment 19*, 2, 107–113.

Caldwell, M.F. (2010) 'Study characteristics and recidivism base rates in juvenile sex offender recidivism.' *International Journal of Offender Therapy and Comparative Criminology 54*, 2, 197–212.

Carpentier, M., Silovsky, J.F. and Chaffin, M. (2006) 'Randomized trial of treatment for children with sexual behaviour problems: Ten year follow up.' *Journal of Consulting and Clinical Psychology 74*, 3, 482–488.

Chaffin, M. (2008) 'Our minds are made up – don't confuse us with the facts: Commentary on policies concerning children with sexual behaviour problems and juvenile sex offenders.' *Child Maltreatment 13*, 2, 110.

Chaffin, M., Berliner, L., Block, R., Johnson, T.C, *et al.* (2008) 'Report of the ATSA task force on children with sexual behavior problems.' *Child Maltreatment 13*, 2, 199–218.

Christodoulides, T.E., Richardson, G., Graham, F., Kennedy, P.J. and Kelly, T.P. (2005) 'Risk assessment with adolescent sex offenders.' *Journal of Sexual Aggression 11*, 1, 37–48.

Clark, M.D. (2013) 'The Strengths Perspective in Criminal Justice.' In D. Saleebey (ed.) *The Strengths Perspective in Social Work Practice*, 6th ed. Boston, MA: Allyn and Bacon.

Cossins, A. (2000) *Masculinities, Sexualities and Child Sexual Abuse.* The Hague, Netherlands: Kluwer Law International.

Craig, L.A., Browne, K.D., Stringer, I. and Beech, A. (2005) 'Sexual recidivism: A review of static, dynamic and actuarial predictors.' *Journal of Sexual Aggression* 11, 1, 65–84.

Criminal Justice Joint Inspection (2013) *Examining Multi-Agency Responses to Children and Young People Who Sexually Offend: A Joint Inspection of the Effectiveness of Multi-agency Work with Children and Young People in England and Wales who have Committed Sexual Offences and Were Supervised in the Community.* Available at www.justice.gov.uk/downloads/publications/inspectorate-reports/hmiprobation/joint-thematic/children-yp-who-sexually-offend-report.pdf, accessed on 5 August 2014.

Dalrymple, J. and Burke, B. (1995) *Anti-oppressive Practice, Social Care and the Law.* Buckingham, UK: Open University Press.

Day, K. (1993) 'Crime and Mental Retardation.' In K. Howells and H. Hollin (eds) *Clinical Approaches to the Mentally Disordered Offender.* Chichester, UK: Wiley.

Department of Health (DoH) (1988) *Protecting Children: A Guide for Social Workers Undertaking a Comprehensive Assessment* [known as the 'Orange Book']. London, UK: HMSO.

Department for Children, Schools and Families (DCSF) (2010) *Working Together to Safeguard Children, A guide to inter-agency working to safeguard and promote the welfare of children.* London, UK: DCSF Publications.

Department of Health (DoH) (1991) *Working Together under the Children Act 1989: A Guide to Arrangements for Inter-agency Co-operation for the Protection of Children from Abuse.* London, UK: HMSO.

Department of Health (DoH) (1992) *A Strategic Statement on Working with Abusers.* London, UK: DoH.

Department of Health (DoH) (1995) *Messages from Research.* London, UK: HMSO.

Department of Health (DoH) (1999) *Working Together to Safeguard Children: A Guide to Inter-agency Working to Safeguard and Promote the Welfare of Children.* London, UK: The Stationery Office.

Department of Health (DoH) (2000) *Framework for the Assessment of Children and their Families,* London, UK: The Stationery Office.

Early, T. and GlenMaye, L.F. (2000) 'Valuing families: Social work practice with families from a strengths perspective.' *Social Work 45*, 2, 118–130.

Edwards, L.M. and Pedrotti, J.T. (2004) 'Utilizing the strengths of our cultures. Therapy with biracial women and children.' *Women and Therapy 27*, 1–2, 33–43.

Elliott, M. (1985) *Preventing Child Sexual Abuse: A Practical Guide to Talking with Children.* London, UK: Bedford Square Press.

Epston, D. (1998) *Catching up with David Epston: A Collection of Narrative-based Papers, 1991–1996.* Adelaide, Australia: Dulwich Centre Publications.

Essex, S. and Gumbleton, J. (1999) '"Similar but different" conversations: Working with denial in cases of severe child abuse.' *Australian and New Zealand Journal of Family Therapy 20*, 3, 139–148.

Fehrenbach, P., Smith, W., Monastersky, C. and Deisher, R. (1986) 'Adolescent sex offenders: Offender and offense characteristics.' *American Journal of Orthopsychiatry 56*, 2, 225–233.

Finklehor, D. (1984) *Child Sexual Abuse: New Theory and Research.* New York, NY: Free Press.

Fisher, D. (1994) 'Adult Sex Offenders: Who Are They? Why and How They Do it.' In T. Morrison, M. Erooga and R.C. Beckett (eds) *Sexual Offending Against Children: Assessment and Treatment of Male Abusers.* London, UK: Routledge.

Flander, G.B., Cosic, I. and Profaca, B. (2009) 'Exposure of children to sexual content on the internet in Croatia.' *Child Abuse and Neglect 33*, 12, 849–856.

Freeman, J., Epston, D. and Lobovits, D. (1997) *Playful Approaches to Serious Problems: Narrative Therapy with Children and Their Families.* London, UK: W.W. Norton.

Friedrich, W.N. (2007) *Children with Sexual Behavior Problems: Family-based, Attachment-focused Therapy.* New York, NY: Norton.

Gilligan, R. (2010) 'Promoting Positive Outcomes in Children in Need.' In: J. Horwath (ed.) *The Child's World: The Comprehensive Guide to Assessing Children in Need.* London, UK: Jessica Kingsley Publishers.

Gray, C. (1991) *The Gray Center for Social Learning and Understanding.* Available at www. thegraycenter.org, accessed 10 April 2014.

Greenland, C. (1987) *Preventing CAN Deaths: An International Study of Deaths Due to Child Abuse and Neglect.* London, UK: Tavistock.

Grubin, D. (1998) *Sex Offending Against Children: Understanding the Risk.* Police Research Series Paper 99. London, UK: Home Office.

Gumbleton, J. (1997) 'Untreatable Families? Working with Denial in Cases of Severe Child Abuse.' Cited in A. Turnell and S. Essex (2008) *Working with 'Denied' Child Abuse: The Resolutions Approach.* Maidenhead, UK: Open University Press.

Hackett, S. (2000) 'Sexual aggression, diversity and the challenge of anti-oppressive practice.' *Journal of Sexual Aggression 5*, 1, 4–20.

Hackett, S. (2004) *What Works for Children and Young People with Sexually Harmful Behaviours?* Barkingside, UK: Barnardo's.

Hackett, S. and Masson, H. (2003) 'A decade on from the NCH Report (1992): Adolescent sexual aggression policy, practice and service delivery across the UK and Republic of Ireland.' *Journal of Sexual Aggression 9*, 2, 109–124.

Hackett, S., Masson, H. and Phillips, S. (2005) *Services for Young People Who Sexually Abuse: A Report on Mapping and Exploring Services for Young People Who Have Sexually Abused Others.* London, UK: Youth Justice Board for England and Wales.

Häggström-Nordin, E., Tydén, T., Hanson, U. and Larsson, M. (2009) 'Experiences of and attitudes towards pornography among a group of Swedish high school students.' *European Journal of Contraception and Reproductive Health Care 14*, 4, 277–284.

Hanson, R.K. (2004) 'Sex Offender Risk Assessment.' In C.R. Hollin (ed.) *The Essential Handbook of Offender Assessment and Treatment.* Chichester, UK: Wiley.

Hardwick, L. (2005) 'Fostering children with sexualised behaviour.' *Adoption and Fostering 29*, 2, 33–43.

HM Government (2010) *Working Together to Safeguard Children: A Guide to Inter-agency Working to Safeguard and Promote the Welfare of Children.* London, UK: DCSF.

Home Office (1997) *No More Excuses: A New Approach to Tackling Youth Crime in England and Wales.* Cm 3809. London, UK: The Stationery Office.

Horvath, A.H.M., Alys, L., Massey, K., Pina, A., Scally, M. and Adler, J.R. (2013) *'Basically… Porn is Everywhere.' A Rapid Evidence Assessment on the Effect that Access and Exposure to Pornography has on Children and Young People.* London, UK: The Office of the Children's Commissioner.

Howe, D. (2008) *The Emotionally Intelligent Social Worker.* Basingstoke, UK: Palgrave.

Hubble, M., Duncan, B. and Miller, S. (1999) *The Heart and Soul of Change: What Works in Therapy.* Washington, DC: American Psychological Association.

Jenkins, A. (1990) *Invitations to Responsibility: The Therapeutic Engagement of Men Who Are Violent and Abusive.* Adelaide, Australia: Dulwich Centre Publications.

Jenkins, A. (1996) 'Moving Towards Respect: A Quest for Balance.' In C. McClean, M. Carey and M. White (eds) *Men's Ways of Being.* Oxford, UK: Westview Press.

Jenkins, A. (2005a) 'Making it Fair: Respectful and Just Intervention with Disadvantaged Young People Who Have Abused.' In M. Calder (ed.) *Children and Young People Who Sexually Abuse. New Theory Research and Practice Developments.* Lyme Regis, UK: Russell House.

Jenkins, A. (2005b) 'Knocking on Shame's Door: Facing Shame Without Shaming Disadvantaged Young People Who Have Abused.' In M. Calder (ed.) *Children and Young People Who Sexually Abuse. New Theory Research and Practice Developments.* Lyme Regis, UK: Russell House.

Johnson, T.C. (1989) 'Female child perpetrators: Children who molest other children.' *Child Abuse and Neglect 13,* 4, 571–585.

Johnson, T.C. (2004) *Helping Children with Sexual Behaviour Problems – A Guidebook for Parents and Substitute Caregivers,* 2nd ed. South Pasadena, CA: Author.

Kahn, T.J. and Chambers, H. (1991) 'Assessing reoffense risk with juvenile sexual offenders.' *Child Welfare LXX,* 3, 333–345.

Lane, S. (1991) 'The Sexual Abuse Cycle.' In G. Ryan and S. Lane (eds) *Juvenile Sexual Offending: Causes, Consequences and Corrections,* 1st ed. Lexington, MA: Lexington Books.

Lane, S. (1997) 'The Sexual Abuse Cycle.' In G. Ryan and S. Lane (eds) *Juvenile Sexual Offending: Causes, Consequences and Corrections,* 2nd ed. San Francisco, CA: Jossey-Bass.

Lane, S. and Zamora, P. (1982, 1984) cited in S. Lane (1997) 'The Sexual Abuse Cycle.' In G. Ryan and S. Lane (eds) *Juvenile Sexual Offending: Causes, Consequences and Corrections,* 2nd ed. San Francisco, CA: Jossey-Bass.

Longo, R. and Calder, M. (2005) 'The Use of Sex Offender Registration with Young People Who Sexually Abuse.' In M. Calder (eds) *Children and Young People Who Sexually Abuse.* Dorset, UK: Russell House.

Luthar, S., Cicchetti, D. and Becker, B. (2000) 'The construction of resilience: A critical evaluation and guidelines for future work.' *Child Development 71,* 3, 543–562.

Masson, H. (1995) 'Children and adolescents who sexually abuse other children: Responses to an emerging problem.' *Journal of Social Welfare and Family Law 17,* 3, 325–336.

McCann, K. and Lussier, P. (2008) 'Antisocial, sexual deviance, and sexually reoffending in juvenile sex offenders: A meta-analytic investigation.' *Youth Violence and Juvenile Justice 6,* 4, 363–385.

McCrory, E. (2010) *A Treatment Manual for Adolescents Displaying Harmful Sexual Behaviour: Change for Good.* London, UK: Jessica Kingsley Publishers.

Miller, W.R., Benefield, R.G. and Tonnigan, J.S. (1993) 'Enhancing motivation for change in problem drinking: A controlled comparison of two therapist styles.' *Journal of Consulting and Clinical Psychology 61,* 3, 455–461.

Miller, W.R. and Rollnick, S. (2002) *Motivational Interviewing: Preparing People for Change,* 2nd ed. New York, NY: Guilford Press.

Milner, J. (2006) 'From stigma and isolation to strength and solidarity: parents talking about their experiences of caring for children whose behaviour has been sexually concerning or harmful.' *International Journal of Narrative Therapy and Community Work 2,* 53–60.

Milner, J. (2008) 'Solution-focused approaches to caring for children whose behaviour is sexually harmful.' *Adoption and Fostering 32,* 4, 42–50.

Milner, J. and Bateman, J. (2011) *Working with Children and Teenagers using Solution Focused Approaches: Enabling Children to Overcome Challenges and Achieve Their Potential.* London, UK: Jessica Kingsley Publishers.

Morrison, T. (1996) 'Making an impact: Where next with adolescents who sexually abuse?' Keynote speech at *Learning to Change* Barnardo's Conference, 14 March 1996, Liverpool Town Hall, Liverpool, UK.

Morrison, T., Erooga, M. and Beckett, R.C. (1994) *Sexual Offending against Children: Assessment and Treatment of Male Abusers.* London, UK: Routledge.

Munro, E. (2011) *The Munro Review of Child Protection. Interim Report: The Child's Journey.* London, UK: Department for Education.

Myers, S. and Milner, J. (2007) *Sexual Issues in Social Work.* Bristol, UK: Policy Press.

Myers, S. with McLaughlin, M. and Warwick, K. (2003) 'The day the touching monster came: Narrative and solution focused approaches to working with children and young people with sexually inappropriate behaviour.' *Journal of Educational Psychology 20,* 1, 76–89.

REFERENCES

National Children's Home (NCH) (1992) *The Report of the Committee of Enquiry into Children and Young People Who Sexually Abuse Other Children.* London, UK: NCH.

NOTA National Committee on Adolescents Who Sexually Harm (2003) *Response to Protecting the Public-Strengthening Protection against Sex Offenders and Reforming the Law on Sexual Offences,* cited in H. Masson (2006) 'Policy, Law and Organisational Contexts in the United Kingdom, Ongoing Complexity and Change.' In M. Erooga and H. Masson (eds) *Children and Young People Who Sexually Abuse Others, Current Developments and Practice Responses,* 2nd ed. New York, NY: Routledge.

NSPCC (2013) *Safeguarding in Education Service. Briefing: The Role of Schools, Colleges and Academies in Recognising and Supporting Children who Display Harmful Sexual Behaviour.* Available at www.nspcc.org.uk/Inform/resourcesforteachers/good-practice/Recognising%20and%20supporting%20children%20who%20display%20harmful%20sexual%20behaviour_wdf98415.pdf, accessed on 30 September 2014.

O'Callaghan, D. and Print, B. (1994) 'Adolescent Sexual Abusers: Research, Assessment and Treatment.' In T. Morrison, M. Erooga and R.C. Beckett (eds) *Sexual Offending against Children: Assessment and Treatment of Male Abusers.* London, UK: Routledge.

Ofsted (2010) *The Safe Use of New Technologies.* Manchester, UK: Ofsted.

Papadopoulos, L. (2010) *Sexualisation of Young People: Review.* London, UK: Home Office.

Parton, C. (1990) 'Women, Gender Oppression and Child Abuse.' In The Violence Against Children Study Group (eds) *Taking Child Abuse Seriously.* London, UK: Routledge.

Payne, M. (2006) *Narrative Therapy,* 2nd ed. London, UK: Sage.

Polaschek, D.L.L. (2001) 'Relapse prevention: Offense process models an the treatment of sexual offenders.' *Journal of Interpersonal Violence 6,* 523–544.

Quillam, S. (2005) '"Teen mags": Helpful or harmful?' *Journal of Family Planning and Reproductive Health Care 31,* 1, 77–79.

Rapp, C.A. (1998) *The Strengths Model: Case Management with People Suffering from Severe and Persistent Mental Illness.* New York, NY: Oxford University Press.

Reitzel, L.R. and Carbonell, J.L. (2006) 'The effectiveness of sexual offender treatment for juveniles as measured by recidivism: A meta-analysis.' *Sexual Abuse: Journal of Research and Treatment 18,* 401–421.

Reivich, K. and Shatte, A. (2003) *The Resilience Factor: 7 Keys to Finding Your Inner Strength and Overcoming Life's Hurdles.* London, UK: Broadway Books.

Reynhout, G. and Carter, M. (2006). 'Social stories for children with disabilities'. *Journal of Autism and Developmental Disorders 36,* 445–469.

Richardson, G. (2005) 'Early maladaptive schemas in a sample of British adolescent sexual abusers: Implications for therapy.' *Journal of Sexual Aggression 11,* 259–276.

Ryan, G. and Blum, J. (1994). *Childhood Sexuality, A Guide for Parents.* Denver, CO: Kempe Center.

Ryan, G., Miyoshi, T.J., Metzner, J.L., Krugman, R.D. and Fryer, G.E. (1996) 'Trends in a national sample of sexually abusive youths.' *Journal of the American Academy of Child and Adolescent Psychiatry 33,* 17–25.

Ryan G. and Lane, S. (1997) 'Introduction.' In G. Ryan and S. Lane (eds) *Juvenile Sexual Offending: Causes, Consequences, and Correction.* San Francisco, CA: Jossey-Bass.

Saleebey, D. (ed.) (2007) *The Strengths Perspective in Social Work Practice,* 4th ed. Boston, MA: Allyn and Bacon.

Saleebey, D. (2013) 'Introduction: Power in the People.' In D. Saleebey (ed.) *The Strengths Perspective in Social work Practice,* 6th ed. Boston, MA: Allyn and Bacon.

Sampson, R.J. and Laub, J.H. (2005) 'A life course view of the development of crime.' *Annals of the American Academy of Political and Social Science 602,* 12–45.

Saunders, E.B. and Awad, G.A. (1988) 'Assessment, management, and treatment planning for male adolescent sexual offenders.' *American Journal of Orthopsychiatry 58,* 4, 571–579.

Selekman, M.D. (2002) *Living on the Razor's Edge.* London, UK and New York, NY: Norton.

Selekman, M.D. (2007) *The Optimistic Child: A Proven Program to Safeguard Children against Depression and Build Lifelong Resilience.* New York, NY: Houghton Mifflin.

Shazer, S. de (1985) *Keys to Solution in Brief Therapy*. New York, NY: W.W. Norton.

Shazer, S. de (1988) *Clues: Investigating Solutions in Brief Therapy*. New York, NY: W.W. Norton.

Shazer, S. de (1991) *Putting Difference to Work*. New York, NY: W.W. Norton.

Silovsky, J.F., Niec, L., Bard, D. and Hecht, D. (2007) 'Treatment for preschool children with sexual behaviour problems: Pilot study.' *Journal of Clinical Child and Adolescent Psychology 36*, 378–391.

Skrypek, M., Idzelis, M. and Pecora, P.J. (2012) 'Signs of Safety in Minnesota: Parent perceptions of a Signs of Safety child protection experience.' Wilder Research. Available at http://cssr.berkeley.edu/cwscmsreports/LatinoPracticeAdvisory/PRACTICE_EB_Child_Welfare_Practice_Models/Safety%20Organized%20Practice/Skrypek%202012.pdf, accessed on 5 August 2014.

Speirs, F. (Undated) Autism and ADHD Information. Available at www.fionaspeirs.co.uk, accessed on 18 November 2014.

Thompson, N. (2003) *Language and Communication*. Basingstoke, UK: Palgrave.

Turnell, A. (2012) *The Signs of Safety: Comprehensive Briefing Paper*. Victoria Park, WA: Resolutions Consultancy.

Turnell, A. and Edwards, S. (1999) *Signs of Safety: A Solution and Safety Oriented Approach to Child Protection*. New York, NY: W.W. Norton.

Turnell, A. and Essex, S. (2006) *Working with 'Denied' Child Abuse: The Resolutions Approach*. Maidenhead: Open University Press.

UK Children's Commissioners (2008) *UK Children's Commissioners' Report to the UN Committee on the Rights of the Child*. Available at www.niccy.org/uploaded_docs/uncrc_report_final.pdf, accessed 5 August 2014.

Vivian-Byrne, S.E. (2002) 'Using context and difference in sex offender treatment: An integrated approach.' *Journal of Sexual Aggression 8*, 59–73.

Ward, T. (2002) 'Good lives and the rehabilitation of offenders: Promises and problems.' *Aggression and Violent Behaviour 7*, 5, 513–528.

Ward, T. and Mann, R.E. (2004) 'Good Lives and the Rehabilitation of Offenders: A Positive Approach to Treatment.' In P.A. Linley and S. Joseph (eds) *Positive Psychology in Practice*. Hoboken, NJ: John Wiley.

Ward, T. and Stewart, C.A. (2003) 'The treatment of sex offenders: Risk management and good lives.' *Professional Psychology: Research and Practice 34*, 4, 353–360.

Ward, T., Mann, R.E. and Gannon, T.A. (2007) 'The good lives model of offender rehabilitation: Clinical implications.' *Aggression and Violent Behavior 12*, 87–107.

Wheeler, J. (2005) 'Solution focused training for social workers.' In T. Nelson (ed.) *Education and Training in Solution Focused Brief Therapy*. New York, NY: The Haworth Press.

White, M. (1989) *Selected Papers*. Adelaide: Dulwich Centre Newsletter.

White, M. (1993) 'Deconstruction and Therapy.' In S. Gilligan and R. Price (eds) *Therapeutic Conversations*. New York, NY and London, UK: W.W. Norton.

White, M. (1995) *Re-authoring Lives: Interviews and Essays*. Adelaide, Australia: Dulwich Centre Publications.

White, M. (1996) Verbal Communications. Conference on Narrative Practice. Doncaster, UK.

White, M. and Epston, D. (1990) *Narrative Means to Therapeutic Ends*. New York, NY: Norton.

Wolf, S.C. (1984) 'A multifactorial model of deviant sexuality.' Paper presented at Third International Conference on Victimology. Lisbon, Spain.

Worling, J.R. and Curwen, T. (2000) 'Adolescent sexual offender recidivism: Success of specialized treatment and implications for risk prediction.' *Child Abuse and Neglect 24*, 7, 965–982.

Wylie, L.A. and Griffin, H.L. (2013) 'G-map's application of the Good Lives Model to adolescent males who sexually harm: A case study.' *Journal of Sexual Aggression 19*, 345–356.

Youth Justice Board (YJB) (2008) *Key Elements of Effective Practice: Young People Who Sexually Abuse*. London, UK: Youth Justice Board for England and Wales.

SUBJECT INDEX

AUTHOR INDEX